Rhythmic Ramblings

C Scott PHD

Rhythmic Ramblings

Copyright © 2017 by C Scott PHD

All rights reserved. No part of this book may be reproduced or transmitted in any form or by any means without written permission from the author.

Cover art provided by: Alyssa Besly

ISBN (978-0-9973435-1-9)

Table of Contents

The Reason 9
Grow Up 10
Cougar 12
Questions 14
Pain 16
The Mistress 18
They 20
Sick 21
Just a Man 23
Delusional 26
Mother 27
Plastics 29
T O Y 31
Tears of a Warrior 32
The Doll 34
I Write 38
His Wife 39
Strings 41
I Just Don't Know Anymore 43
Issues 44
Stranger Danger 46
Garden Help 48
Thief 50
Caged 53
How Much Longer 54
The Set-up 56
Nobody at All 58
Not Satisfied 60
No One 62

Original	64
No Approval Needed	65
Broke	68
My Ship	70
Daddy's Little Girl	71
Flying Solo	74
Paper	76
The Difference	77
Cubic	79
I Wish	81
Phoenix	82
Another Man's Wife	84
Cougar's Last Dance	86
Party Time	88
Oasis	91
Butterfly	93
Small Circle	95
Diamonds	97
The Things They Carried	98
Copycats	101
Skewed	103
Stop the Madness	104
What If?	106
You Say	108
Remember Me	109
Fake	111
Dark Night	113
The Story	115
Reflection	119
Seed	121
Reap	123

Police State	125
Name	127
The Secret	128
Lonely Road	130
Alive	131
Whipped	132
Lies	134
Fool	136
Tears	137
Cavemen	138
Drinking Sand	139
Side Piece	141
Please	143
I Know	144
I Need a Man	145
The Greatest Commandment	147
Charm	149
Sweep	151
Contradictions	153
Mind	154
Just Like You	156
Thank You	157
Free	159
Mr. Ego	161
Willie Lynch Nation	162
Symptoms of a Married Man	165
The Disease	166
Play	168
Lesson Learned	170
Stone	171
Melting Pot	172

Internalized 174
The Journey 176
Scared 178
Reminder 180
Elite 181
Her Story.. 183
The Rule 185

The Reason

I don't write to impress
I write to undress
The pieces of my soul
When I use my pen it releases
The glue that takes my pieces
And makes me whole
Let me put it to you like this
This pen is my therapist
The pad is my couch
I can release the pain of my past
Without spending a lot of cash
I will write til my ink runs out
I don't care if you know my name
This isn't about fortune or fame
I still write while broke
Even though I make you smile
Every once in a while
Please believe this is not a joke
You don't have to like my words
That's not the worse that I've heard
I don't write to please
When I put pen to paper and do what I do
I don't write for anyone especially you
I write to release what's in me

Grow Up

How old are you
I really can't tell right now
You dress like you need a manager every time you go out
You talk like a teenager but look like you deserve a discount at Denny's
Wearing enough make-up to cover every female that attended the Emmy's
And to the men
I'm talking to you too
Rolling around in a car that costs more than ALL of your kids' schools
Pants hanging around your butt like belts are against your beliefs
Listening to music that would give your grandmother grief
Do you think that stuff is sexy
That you'll catch somebody quicker
That's almost as dumb as thinking you can walk a straight line after drinking gallons of liquor
Would you PLEASE grow up and act your age
You're not getting paid for this
You are NOT on stage
There's no profit to it and it can't be that much fun
Pretending to be pretty smart and looking VERY dumb
Trying to figure out what's wrong in the world and the picture's not getting any clearer
Have you ever thought the problem might be staring back at you from the mirror
Who's teaching your kids to be adults if you're acting just like them
Since when did being a parent mean you have to be their friend
It's our job to teach them how to function in this world

Not how to run game on some little boy or girl
But hey why am I talking
You're not going to listen to me
Unless I can convince Lil Wayne to put this on his next CD

Cougar

She stood in the shadows and prepared for her prowl
The music was so loud no one heard her soft growl
The herd was thick
There was an abundance of prey
She could have some tonight
And there'd still be more the next day
Into the room she stepped
The hunt had began
She was looking for a boy she could make think he was a man
This was nothing new to her
She had done it all before
Once her victim fell in love
She quickly became bored
Love was not her destination
Nowhere near her goal
She just wanted a warm body to keep her bed from getting cold
Her unsuspecting victims all thought they knew the game
They bragged about imaginary conquests
Made all sorts of claims
But she could see through the nonsense
She'd been around a while
She was much more experienced and covered her age with her style
Her four inch heels and the dress that looked painted on
Had every man in the room wishing they could figure out her song
The one that they could request that would get her to dance
Or maybe they should offer her a drink
Anything to get their chance

She saw the hunger in their eyes and knew exactly what they thought
They didn't realize that they were the fish that she had already caught
She picked one from the crowd and gave him a sexy wink
All common sense left him and the little head began to think
While he was thinking he'd hit the jackpot
Won the grand prize
She was hoping he was worth the trouble and she'd be satisfied
Maybe she'd keep him around
If he was a good little boy
If not
She'd throw him away
And go hunting for another toy
Men aren't the only ones out there looking for young goods
And cougars don't always live in the mountains
Or the woods

Questions

Are all men crazy
Or just the ones that I meet
I can blink and they go to bitter
From sweet

Are they born bi-polar
Or is it something they learn
I wish Dr. Jekyll would tell me when it's almost Mr. Hyde's turn

Are all men intimidated by a woman who thinks for herself
It's not really a relationship if you have to think for someone else

Are all men Neanderthals
I thought cavemen were extinct
I know how to use my brain
I do not need you to think

Do all men have to go through that playa stage
I would think that stuff would get old after a certain age

Why do they expect us to be forgiving when they are not
They remember everything and we're supposed to have memory block

Why is it that when they're busted
They still won't tell the truth
I'm showing you a video boy
What do you mean I don't have proof

Why can't they just admit to the crime and pay the cost
It's better than lying
Which just adds to the time and trust already lost

Who said it was acceptable to sow those oats that are called wild
I think it's just an excuse for a man to remain a child

Why is it that when a man cries
He's considered soft or a punk
God made man in His image so that's a bunch of junk

Who said that men should keep all of their emotions inside
Men have lost so much
All for the sake of their pride

These are just a few of the questions that I sometime ask myself
But since I don't expect any answers
I guess I'll just put this on the shelf

Pain

Whatever happened to shotgun weddings
Protecting our daughters' virtue
Nowadays
Daddy's at home hoping baby girl will bring home a friend he can screw
Instead of parents protecting the innocent
They're selling it for crack rims or rent
I know I know
I'm preaching again
But I'm tired of these kids losing
I want to help them win
Win back their joy
Maybe a little peace of mind
I'll stand up for them
I'll give them my time
Somebody has to do it or it won't get done
A flood starts
With raindrop number one
And after the flow has stopped
There has been a definite change
The fact that some people condone this madness
To me
Is quite strange
You dress your girls like prostitutes before they start to bloom
Then want to act surprised when you catch a boy in their room
And since when is it ok for a little boy to have sex and watch porn
A male teenage virgin has to deal with all sorts of ridicule and scorn
But there is something that his sexually active buddies won't admit

And that's that the few seconds of pleasure are rarely worth it
That it's really not just a bunch of fun and games
That there's no one to tell about the confusion and shame
How did this happen
Where did we lose our way
Is there a chance for our children to have a brighter day
Or will they forever be enslaved by their lust
Boys who can't become men
Girls who don't know who to trust
We have to save this generation
Or there'll be no hope for the next
Yes
There is pleasure
But let's teach them about the pain of sex

The Mistress

I say
Baby it's raining
You know the effect that has
He says
Give me a minute babe
Let me finish this draft
That minute turned to hours
The fire was gone
I forgot
I become the mistress when football season comes home
And this is definitely its home
Even more than mine
Because my man gives it all of his attention
All of his time
Pre-game
The game
Then the commentary shows
To get some attention
I have to walk around with no clothes
I have to be aggressive
I can't drop hints at all
Because the only thing being caught around here
Is a football
I thought I was priority one but now I get the leftover time
Now that football season is here
My husband is no longer mine
He belongs to his team
Both real and fantasy
So I have to find other things to keep me happy

There's no feeling like spending quality time with my man
But he's a slave to football and must do what it commands
Ignore your wife
You can't miss a single play
I am more important
Is what football likes to say
And he listens
He does what he's told
While I am left alone
And the fire grows cold
He's addicted
But refuses rehabilitation
I have to catch him before the game if I want a conversation
This annual obsession of his causes me much distress
Because football becomes the wife and I
Am just
The mistress

They

Watch who you talk to
Watch what they say
They might only be your friend for that day
When you start talking about the problems that you have
They might just be looking for a real good laugh
And even before your mouth is completely closed
They'll be running around telling everyone they know
And the ones that they tell don't really care for you
They'll just run out and do the same thing too
And when you finally hear about it
They've completely rearranged it
Nobody knows why these things are done
They obviously think it's a lot of fun
But you shouldn't worry too much about them
They always get theirs in the end
So take my advice and quickly turn and run the other way
When someone opens their mouth and you hear the word
They

Sick

You're on the outside looking in so please shut up
You have no idea the amount of drama that fills my cup
On the daily
While you only see what you want to see
Stop telling him what you would do if you were me
Because you don't know what you'd do in a situation until you're in it
And I promise you wouldn't put up with this crap for one minute
Just because he's handsome and can make you laugh
Doesn't mean he's perfect
You don't know the half
He's done enough dirt to fill a beach with sand
It takes more than a good body and sexy smile to make a good man
And a big dick doesn't make a good lover
Just in case you didn't know
Stop chasing behind my man
It makes you look like a desperate ho
Yeah
I called you a ho
That's how you act
Running behind my man
Offering him your cat
Your ass
And your mouth too
Offering him everything so he'll come to you
Isn't there some single dude that you can follow around
Or is it that you like looking like a clown
Being laughed at by his friends
And yours

Because you always have zero when they tally up the scores
You're just a stalker who wants to be the side chick
Go play in traffic
Chicks like you make me sick

Just a Man

Sitting here watching the trees dance
Wondering if I ever really had a chance
Was this really possible
Was it ever true
Or was I dreaming
As dreamers often do
Dreaming that
For you
I'd actually be enough
But some habits are hard to break
Some vices too hard to give up
I get it now though
I finally understand
You'll never change
You're not that type of man
You'll always want more
You'll never be satisfied
Your feelings won't be affected by the tears that I've cried
Your pride is more important to you than my heart will ever be
With all the other women you have
Why do you need me
They don't mind sharing
Which is something I don't like to do
Although I've been forced to
Ever since I've been with you
Everyone said it wouldn't work
That we were doomed from the start
But I still took that chance and gave you my heart
You don't appreciate the blessing God has given you by His grace

Instead you get distracted by every sob story or pretty face
I may have a sob story but I don't want a superman
Jesus already saved me
From you
I wanted a wedding band
But that's too much to ask
You putting up your cape
You fight other's battles so your own problems you can escape
And I was willing to fight for us
Even if it meant fighting you
But now I'm all fought out
There's no more I can do
Except tell you I love you and step out of your way
You don't need me to keep you from saving the day
So you keep running from your problems while trying to save everyone else
You'll never be happy until you deal with the issues within yourself
You've been trying to push me away since you first felt my love
Because you don't think you're worthy of a gift from Heaven above
And maybe you're not
But that's just how God works
Showering us with blessings regardless to past hurts
And we've all hurt Him at some point in our lives
Cutting deeper with our sin than a million knives
So the enemy said you don't deserve the gift
And you believed his lies
And the very gift God told you was good
You've come to despise
I can't help you with that

You need to fix this on your own
You want to remain a child while your problems are all grown
I hate throwing in the towel
I've never been one to give in
But I refuse to keep fighting a battle that I know I can't win
You're just a lost boy
Something like Peter Pan
Going around playing superhero instead of just being a man
Maybe one day you'll get it and you'll finally settle down
Unless
Of course
All your adoring fans are nowhere to be found
Once you've saved everyone and you're all used up
How many will be around to just put water in your cup
Or give you a kind word
Maybe just a smile
Probably not many
'Cause by then
You'll be out of style
And you'll have pushed away all the ones who truly cared
Expecting them to sit and wait for you even though you're never there
Hopefully you'll get it before it's too late and you'll finally understand
Only Jesus can save and you
Are just a man

Delusional

Land of the free
Home of the brave
Unless
Of course
You're the descendant of a slave
Or
Maybe your ancestors owned a few
But that's not what people see when they look at you
If you don't have to go out and pay for a tan
There are those who
With pleasure
Your destruction plan
It's not your fault
You've done nothing wrong
It's just that their ignorance and hatred are strong
They try to keep us down with inferior education
Doing their best to make sure we never make it to graduation
Then
If you do go further and get some letters behind your name
There are those that play the overqualified game
I know that not everyone is racist
Get that out of your head
But you're delusional if you believe that racism is dead

Mother

I will be dead and gone one day
But until then
You have to do what I say
Simply because of the fact that I raised you
You have to do what I tell you to
I don't care that you're grown and want your own life
I'll make you miserable
Even after I've picked your husband or wife
See
It's not about love
It's all about control
You don't like God because I've always played that role
Since the day you were born I made you worship me
So that when you were grown
You'd be who I told you to be
I made you feel guilty about things you had nothing to do with
See
You're my slave and the guilt is my whip
Whenever I think you're on the verge of breaking lose
I just break out the guilt
Pour on the emotional abuse
You've broken many hearts
Including the one that beats in your own chest
Just because at manipulation
I
Am the best
You can't imagine the pleasure that it brings
Watching you jump when I pull the strings

You've spent your whole life trying to fix something that you didn't break
And gone financially and emotionally broke trying to replace something that
You didn't take
I could care less about the impossibility of the task
Because I know you'll do it
I will quickly ask
Give up your hopes and dreams
Just a shell of a man
Throw away your chance at love
Give someone you don't want your hand
As long as I'm happy
I'm not concerned about any other
I deserve all of this
Just because you call me mother

Plastics

Impostors
Pretending to be satisfied
Unhappy
Yet won't swallow their pride
And admit
Things aren't how they thought it would be
Just left the office after surgery number three
Had to get the nose done
The implants came from visit number one
Might have skin cancer from too much sun
Or maybe from its lack
Don't want to be too pale
Or too black
Have to look like the girls in the magazines
That's the only way to be seen
Or heard
Or paid attention to
You'll be ignored if you just look like you
That's the lesson taught around the world
To millions of impressionable boys and girls
Beauty is a certain size and skin tone
If they don't fit the mold leave them alone
Lives destroyed in the quest for perfection
Women dying after getting butt injections
Implants burst at the most inopportune times
Yet you get overlooked if you don't buy that line
At least that's what we're taught to believe
But that's just another way to deceive
The masses

Make them unhappy with themselves
So they can choose eyes and asses off of shelves
Not everybody was meant to be a size three
And I don't mind if she doesn't look like me
Or if he doesn't like my size
I'm beautiful in my own eyes
If I don't love me
No one else will
If I'm suicidal
There are other ways to kill
Myself
Than painful side effects
From surgeries implants or injections
That don't protect me from rejection
Never thought I could be accepted
Turned from the One who would have protected
Me
Loved me unconditionally
Drowned out His voice with radio and TV
Forgot that I was one of a kind
Now I'm just another Barbie
With a plastic mind

T O Y

I must admit that this is new to me
Wanting to be with someone that I can't even see
Not really caring that our bodies can't touch
The thought alone
Sometimes
For me is too much
I can see us being together til death do us part
Without me ever
Too seriously
Considering driving a stake through your heart
I can see me being faithful without giving it a second thought
Just because I don't want to hurt you
Not that I'm scared of getting caught
I don't know how you feel whenever I cross your mind
But I hope it's something close
At least some of the time
I think I've said too much
So now I'm through
I just wanted you to know that I was Thinking Of You

Tears of a Warrior
Based on the painting "The Worst Sight" by Kevin A Williams

What could make a warrior cry
What could bring tears to a queen's eye
A vision of what's to come for their future generations
Of them being scattered across the globe
Shunned by every nation
But what really causes a king and queen to lose sleep
That makes that strong warrior fall to his knees and weep
Is not brought on by the slave ship's sight
Or even the sounds of screams from kidnapping in the night
But
The knowledge that there will come a time
When their children will be prisoners in their own mind
When they won't know their own value or worth
And
Some will be ashamed of the race of their birth
When they will believe the lies told by ignorant men
And fall so low that they don't want to get up again
When his sons will kill each other for sport
Or profit
And his daughters will be exploited and abused
But no one will stop it
Why wouldn't a vision like that make him drop to his knees
Knowing that his children will kill each other like rats fighting over cheese
He knows it would be better to be eaten in the jungle
To just die quick
Instead of being walking zombies
Not even knowing that they're sick

He knows the lies that will be told by the kidnappers and thieves
So the tears are for where they're going
Not the home his seed leaves
He knows the hatred that these so called civilized men bare
So he cries
Because he has no way to make his children aware

The Doll

There once was a doll up on a shelf
She had climbed there
All by herself
See
It was too painful down on the floor
So
She decided that she didn't want to play anymore
She climbed up high
And tried to hide
Blocked out all the pain
Pushed it deep inside
Then he came along and noticed her there
He tried to keep walking but
Couldn't help but stare
He reached for her
She shied away
It was familiar there
And she wanted to stay
But he saw the value in her
So he persisted
She had been hurt enough and strongly resisted
But He was determined and turned on the charm
Swore that he was different
That he meant no harm
She gave in
Put herself within his reach
And prayed that
This unspoken contract
He would not breach

But that prayer went unanswered and pain came quick
See
She was just another conquest
He had just been talkin' slick
He wanted her to stay on the shelf
But no longer out of sight
To watch him play all day
And be ready for him at night
For a while she tried
Pretended it didn't hurt
It got to a point that she couldn't see him
For all of his dirt
And yet
She held on
Like a good little doll
Stayed in her lane
Answered every call
Silently watching as he played with toy
After toy
Hoping he'd finally grow to a man
From a boy
She saw his potential
The life he could claim
But he couldn't see it
And that was a shame
While he was playing and moving his toys all around
She had started climbing back up and was far off the ground
You see
She had decided it was safer on the shelf
Away from prying eyes
That it was better to put on a mask

Wear a disguise
A disguise that said
I don't need love
It's useless and outdated
Kind of like an old movie
Under viewed and overrated
He was so busy playing
He didn't see what was going on
Until the day he looked around and his favorite doll was gone
He looked where he had found her
But she knew better than to hide there
He could have found her if he had searched
But he really didn't care
There were so many other dolls that were blocking his view
That he forgot all his promises
All he'd said he would do
Like a spoiled kid
He wanted to claim that the doll was at fault
That he had tried his best
And didn't deserve her verbal assault
He knew that wasn't the case
But he would never admit the truth
He didn't really want one doll
And that was his best excuse
He wanted to be able to play with every toy in the store
He didn't want just one at home he had to protect and provide for
So the doll that was broken
Lost another piece and learned
That she couldn't trust little boys where commitment was concerned
Now

Back on the shelf
She began to collect dust
And wondered if there was anyone she could trust
The Toy Maker came and found her hiding place
Mended her dress
Washed her face
Put together all the pieces that she thought she had lost
Did it all freely
His Son had already paid the cost
When He was done with the repairs
He held her close to His heart
Told her to forget the past
That it was time for a new start
He reassured her that not everyone was like that selfish little boy
And that He would one day entrust her to someone who would bring her great joy
She wanted to believe Him
But it was kind of hard
He had fixed her up
But she still had those old scars
He took her off the workbench and put her on display for the world to see
And whispered
Don't worry my child because
You
Were made
For Me

I Write

I'm hurting so I write
I'm healing so I write
I'm angry so I write
I'm happy so I write
I'm horny so I write
I'm bored so I write
My pen is my therapist my lover my priest
My pad is always there when I need some relief

He died so I write
He lied so I write
She's hurt so I write
She's done dirt so I write
She's been wronged so I write
He took too long so I write
My pen offers comfort to those in need
My pad is the key by which minds are freed

It's raining so I write
They're complaining so I write
It's fun so I write
They won so I write
It's a celebration so I write
There's discrimination so I write
My pen is the tool by which the darkness I fight
My pad is here to keep me sane so I write

His Wife

He's hurting but no one will listen
He's dodgin' but she's still hittin'
And what everybody seems to missin'
Is the point
Of the knife
That will eventually take his life
The attacker
His wife
So he can't call for help
Can't defend himself
Or he'll go to jail
Living in a hell
That he signed up for
Unknowingly
When he
Wedded she
No one understands
Tells him to be a man
And never raise his hand
In self defense
Or anger
Married a stranger
Now he's in real danger
Of losing his life
Can't press charges on his wife
Barely sleeps at night
Because of the fear
And the mocking in his ears
That he still hears

Even when no one is near
So he lies
About the black eyes
Not really surprised
That everyone realized
The truth
When it was of no use
Double homicide
Followed by suicide
Daddy and baby died
She cried
Then tried to hide
In hell
Didn't want a jail cell
Family finally saw the proof
But he lived
And died
With the abuse

Strings

Independents
Democrats
Libertarians
Republicans
More like legalized crooks
Paid con men
Party doesn't matter
Neither does race
Their only goal is keeping you in your place
The laws they write
To them
Do not apply
So when they act concerned
It's all a big lie
They don't care about your issues
Or what you're going through
All they want
Is for their way of life to continue
So they say one thing
And do another
All the while telling you to blame your brother
Your brother in this struggle
This constant fight
Of providing for your family in a way that's legal and right
You want to believe that your candidate's loyalty can't be bought
Because that's not the American way
Or so we've been taught
The truth is
They don't care about party affiliation

As long as they have control in this supposedly great nation
I don't care if you're liberal or conservative
Politicians aren't concerned with how you live
As long as your taxes keep them in designer gear
They'll tell you whatever lie you want to hear
And you want to hear it
That's what you pay them for
They give you reasons to fight and complain just a little more
If you were at peace
Or even slightly satisfied
You'd have time to reflect on how much they've lied
And how many of those lies you gladly upheld
That would cause you more grief than the day the towers fell
So you buy their lies with your children's money
Jumping when they say jump like a good little monkey
I know that you'll ignore the truth that my words bring
Politicians are all puppets
You just don't see the strings

I Just Don't Know Anymore

I really think I love you
I was so sure before
I just don't know what happened
I just don't know anymore

You're always saying you love me
Oh so tender smooth and sweet
But I wonder is it to convince yourself
I all too often wonder is there someone else
I used to be so sure that it was me that you adored
I just don't know what happened
I just don't know anymore

Though we're still together semi-happily
Doubtfully loving one another
How long will it be
Until it's finally over
It would be you and me
We would never part
I believe now it was a fantasy
Deep in my heart
Though I'd lose my mind if you ever walked out that door
I just don't know what happened
I just don't know anymore

Issues

America's going broke and it's a newsworthy scandal
I've been broke for a while yet still manage to handle
My business
And make sure my kids are fed
My life hasn't changed since Osama's supposedly been dead
Yet people were dancing and celebrating in the street
Because America's enemy had reportedly been beat
Really
Are you sure about that
It seems most of our enemies don't wear turbans as hats
Just like the ones that hurt me most share my DNA
Most of America's enemies were born in the good ol' US of A
I won't apologize for saying that
I meant no disrespect
Plus
I could care less about being politically correct
That's why the rate of heart attacks in this country is so high
Why high blood pressure and stroke med 'scripts are to the sky
I could hold it all in
But that wouldn't help me
Like I said
I'm broke
I can't afford therapy
I've got kids to take care of and I do it alone
Because I married a kid that I thought was full grown
Since he let the government screw him with no Vaseline and no tip
On his child support
It's easy for him to skip
People want to complain about families on government aid

But don't think about the money that we've paid
On these wars
And we've taxed businesses into moving overseas
Like I said
We are our own worse enemies
I guess that's just human nature
We must like grief
I've let someone close to me knowing that they were a thief
Maybe not in the literal sense of the word
But there are people that can steal your joy
Just in case you haven't heard
My issues and my country's are actually kind of the same
Because they could all be fixed if we simply call on Jesus' name

Stranger Danger

We told you
Beware of the leeches
With chameleon skills
Who get closer to your skin
Than your shoe to your heels
All the while
Appearing harmless
Plotting all the destruction and mess
They're going to leave
Laughing as you grieve
At all you've lost
Only realizing the cost
When it was too late
Now you sit outside the gate
Of what used to be yours
Saying you won't trust no more
Never again in life
Because you ignored the sounds of the knife
Being sharpened behind your back
Totally unprepared for the attack
Caused by one you called
Friend
So you say
Never again
Claiming you weren't warned
Ye the good advice given
Was scorned
Loved ones were ignored
When they tried

To point out what you'd let into
Your inner circle
Didn't want it
To hurt you
But stubbornness prevailed
And now you sit and wail
As we watch the trail
Of that leech
As it slithers away
Hoping the next one will listen
When others say
Danger
You can't always be kind
To strangers

Garden Help

She said it was his fault
We had it all wrong
We've been blaming the wrong person all along
How could we blame her
When she didn't understand
She was a simple creature
While he was a big
Strong man
She was blinded by the beauty of the object offered
The salesman chose her
Because her brains were softer
She had never used it
It was just there
Her man did the thinking
So she was unaware
If he had been approached first
The salesman would've been clowned
He would've laughed his ass off and knocked the object to the ground
But
That's not how it happened
So he gets almost no blame
While his lady gets a lot of negative press and unwanted fame
If Adam had simply said
Naw baby
I got this
We'd still be running around naked
In a world of constant bliss
But he was lazy

As some of you are today
And wanted her to work
So that he could play
So fellas
Don't be like Adam
And let your girl work in the garden by herself
There may be a snake nearby
Go ahead and give her some help
Or
She may do like Eve
If a slick talker does show
Sell your house for some fruit
Then where will you go
In other words
When your girl says she'll do the chores alone
Pick up a broom and sweep
Or you may lose your comfy home

Thief

Supposed to be giving pleasure
Yet creating pain
I guess it doesn't matter
I still said his name
But only after he threatened my life
And nicked my nipple with his knife
I don't understand
Why my pain excites this man
Why when I fight
It seems to ignite
A fire
I didn't know he had
Reminds me of my dad
Or rather
Something he said
When he used to come to my bed
After momma was asleep
He told me I was made for this
That it was all I was good for
And just like now
My tears only aroused him more
Why is this happening
What did I do
We've only been out a time or two
And never alone
So I can't see
Why this man would want to hurt me
By taking something he could get free somewhere else
I wish my father had taken the box off the shelf

I know they made condoms back then
And I wouldn't have to go through this again and again
Fathers
Uncles
Neighbors
Priests
Are ALL men sex crazed beasts
Or just wolves
And I'm the feast
Do I give off a victim's scent
Were all of my joy coins spent
In another life
Is that why this one's full of strife
Or maybe I'm paying the price
For dirt I did in a previous life
Whatever the reason
I just wish this season
Would end
And I could spend
Just one day
Not feeling this way
What way you say
Dirty
Scared
As if I was totally unprepared
For what it meant to be a woman these days
And all those men's treacherous ways
If God created woman for man
Then why didn't He make them understand
That you can't steal a gift
And the rift

In this planet's spirituality
Is caused by the treatment of me
And other women and girls
Who are used and abused all over the world
Because if I am your helpmeet
And with me your balance is complete
Then you are stealing from yourself
When you take from me

Caged

Running running I have to get out
Have to show them what I'm about
While I'm locked up I have no clout
I need to find a way to make my captors shout

The shouts will open my cell if only a crack
But once I'm out they won't be able to get me back
I'll move faster than an Olympic runner on the track
Once freed I will give them no slack

I've been roaming around in here for days
Making myself known in various ways
They pretend to ignore me as if they're unfazed
If only they knew my power they would be amazed

But locking me up seems to be the style
They'd rather follow the crowd like a blind child
I see the bones of others like me in a growing pile
Because they can't see that freeing us will be worthwhile

I'm starting to fear that I will die like the rest of my kind
That although my captors have eyes they are mentally blind
I've become weak from trying to escape all this time
If you can hear me I beg of you please free your mind

How Much Longer

Somebody tell me what's wrong with nappy hair
Why are some women so extremely scared
To just be how they were made
Somewhere along the way
Black women got played
We've been convinced that
To be beautiful
We had to be like them
That we had to have their hair
Their walk
Their skin
That the darker you were
The deeper your curse
And to be dark AND nappy-headed
Man
That was worse
The sad part about it is
We do it to
We treat each other worse than those other folks do
We pick on each other because of hair and skin tone
Some people won't even date you unless you're red or yellow-boned
We have been convinced that dark skin and naps are signs of an inferior race
So we do all that we can to make sure that our kids will have a lighter face
Why
For what
When will this madness stop

Don't you know that it's only when we come together that we'll rise to the top
These divisions were planted in our minds generations ago
With whips and chains
By men whose skin
Was white as snow
And hearts
As black as midnight on the dark side of the moon
They needed to separate us so that we would dance to their tune
They didn't want us to come together so that we could escape
And generations later
We stand idly by while our daughters are raped
Mentally
And sometimes physically too
By an idea that gives them a distorted view
Of themselves
And their sisters and mothers
That causes them to not respect or trust their fathers or brothers
This needs to stop my people
We have got to do better
How much longer will we live under the curse of the Willie Lynch letter
How much longer will we fight amongst ourselves and keep each other down
While running behind other races and only being seen as a clown
How much longer will we sit around and complain about what others have that we don't
Instead of looking at what they will do that we won't
If we don't acknowledge our weaknesses
Then we can never get stronger
Can somebody please tell me how much longer

The Set-up

What they don't know won't hurt 'em
That's what you say
They forgave me last time
They'll forgive me today
That's a trick of the enemy
To keep you from your blessing
No one that knows their worth will stay somewhere when they're constantly stressing
It won't hurt to have their number
We're just friends is how you justify
But now that the door has been opened
It becomes easier to lie
Trust is like glass
Hard to fix
Easy to break
So if you want it to last
Great care you must take
A secret is like a terminal cancer in any relationship
Like a loose piece of carpet on which
One day
You will trip
Say the wrong thing
Call the wrong name
Then you'll be the loser in your own little game
Somebody told you to go ahead
That the way was clear
But they didn't tell you that you'd probably lose all that you hold dear
Or maybe only some of it

So make sure that it's worth it
You could be miserable for a lifetime over pleasure that only lasted a minute
Some habits
Some addictions
Really aren't worth the price
Neither is that one night stand
So here's a little advice
The next time the enemy wants you to take a sip from his gold-plated cup
Walk away and pray
So that you don't fall
For the set-up

Nobody at All

Nobody's there
Nobody at all
Yet the line's busy every time I call
Wrong number maybe
I don't know
But no one's there
And
I gotta go
Destination unsure
Departure time now
Estimated time of arrival
Somewhere
Somehow
Don't know how to get there
Don't know where there is
But I've been trying to make it since I was a kid
Grown now
According to my age
But that's just a number on a page
No knowledge came with those years
No knob to turn off the tears
No blueprint
Plan
Or map
Don't grow up
It's a trap
Sorry
Wait
Where were we

Oh yes
I was trying to reach my destiny
Will somebody help me
Please answer my call
Nobody's there
Nobody at all

Not Satisfied

Tired of the skin I'm in
Looks too much like my kin
Or maybe
Not enough
Man
This is rough
Not happy with the way I am
Can anyone help
The surgeon can
Nip this
Tuck that
Can't be too thin
Or too fat
Time for the contacts
And the hair dyes
Can never seem to be beautiful
In my own eyes
Lost count of the money I've paid
Fearful of rejection
Wanting to be remade
Perfection at any cost
All faith in the Creator
Lost
Self-esteem has long since hit the hearse
Flat out refuse to believe any verse
That might bring me out of this shade
Didn't like the cards I was dealt
So I played
With a deck of my choosing

Never understanding
That I was losing
The natural beauty
I refused to see
Simply because
I was never satisfied
Being me

No One

You say you can't stand me most of the time
But if someone shows any interest in me
You quickly say
Mine
You pick fights like a gambler trying to pick the winning team
And constantly attempt to crush all of my dreams
I get it
It's over
That's fine by me
Don't get mad that someone else likes what they see
They treasure what you consider trash
All the heartache you gave me will soon be in the past
It was your decision
And I'm no longer upset
What you had with me
Is as good as it gets
You don't see that now
But one day you will
Probably when you are way past over the hill
And realize
That you are all alone
So called friends and family no longer answer the phone
No one to laugh with
Or hold your hand
No one to give you that look that says
Baby
I understand
No one to reach out and touch in the middle of the night
Those are the times that you'll wish that you had done things right

It'll be too late by then
I'll have somewhere else to lay my head
While you're wishing that you could take back some of the things that you said
I'm not trying to change your mind
Believe me
I'm done
And while I'm lying lovingly in their arms
You'll have no one

Original

Those who can do those who can't teach
This is more than just a figure of speech
I could easily stand before a group and recite what I've read
Without ever having an original thought in my head
I could do what I'm told and follow the crowd
Never allowing my own voice to become very loud
But who does that benefit my following you
Copycats don't get the benefits that originals do

Don't stray from the path it's easier that way
You don't need your own voice just say what they say
We don't want pioneers we don't like change
When you try to be different you're viewed as strange
Don't change the music put the CD on repeat
We don't need to dance just shuffle our feet
There's no reason to not be a part of the copycat crew
Because there are so many copycats and originals are few

Why try something different there's nothing left to learn
With innovation and convenience you should not be concerned
Then again where would we be if all the originals had just stopped
If when they met opposition their ideas they just let drop
Some people have been programmed to just accept the status quo
That the world sees you as crazy when you try to find another way to go
Yes change is difficult to accept and painful too
But it is definitely worth it to be the original you

No Approval Needed

Be careful what you wish for
You've often been warned
Yet you still walk around
Acting uninformed
Asking for words that you don't want to hear
Your bravado simply covers your fear
Pretending to be more than what you really are
Which is just a weak batteried flashlight
Wishing on a star
Comparing yourself to heavyweights
Itching to get in the ring
You're gonna get knocked out
That first punch is gonna sting
You don't know what you think you know
You've been lied to
The same ones pumping you up
Are secretly laughing at you
You've been validated by a bunch of hypocritical fakes
I wonder how much more hot air your already inflated head can take
Going around claiming to be a big fish in a small pond
When you're just a minnow
In a muddy hole
That just got pissed on
People tried to stop you
Or at least make you pause
But you heard a sound you mistook for applause
In reality
That sound was the flies gathering around

Because they could smell the bodies that were on the ground
The bodies of the egotistical arrogant ones
Who were left alone to bake in the sun
Their heads were too big for them to get inside
Which they could've fixed
If they had just swallowed their pride
They should've starved that beast
They fed it instead
So eventually they died
From their severely swollen heads
They ignored the warnings just like you have
If it wasn't so sad
I'd probably laugh
I know there are others like you
A few I've even met
But I don't think my resistance to your brand of ignorance is strong enough yet
So I avoid you when I can
Or take you in small doses
Breathe through my hand when you speak
As if you had halitosis
See
I think ignorance is contagious
But I don't know how it's carried
I do know that if I thought like you
I'd already have been buried
Maybe not physically
But intellectually and poetically for sure
Because your special brand of ignorance obviously has no cure
Keep thinking you're a monster
A certified beast

When the big boys come
You won't even be a crumb on the table at their feast
And they won't need your approval when they spit their words
Because a lion getting permission from an ant is just absurd
This may be your final warning
And I hope that it's heeded
When you know what you're called to do
There's no approval needed

Broke

I actually feel sorry for you
Really
I do
Because when you die
No one will mourn you
Your money won't care that you're no longer around
And it won't be there to watch them put you in the ground
It's actually rather sad if you ask me
You sold your soul for a little bit of money
For the love of money is the root of ALL evil
Which is why you spent your life cheating and alienating people
Then you wonder why when you have a need or fall
There's no one around to pick you up or answer your call
Maybe it's because it was clearly understood
That if they were in need
Calling you would do no good
Or
Maybe you cheated them at some point in time
Because keeping your money is always on your mind
You never got married
Not because there wasn't anyone there
But because marriage is a partnership
And your money you refuse to share
No children either
Because they require funds
You wish all your siblings had each only had one
It would cut down on the gifts that you are forced to buy
Christmas
Birthdays

Graduations
They always make you cry
Of course
Not for the same reason as everyone else
Your tears are for the dollars spent you'd rather keep to yourself
You never knew when everyone laughed that you were the joke
Spent your whole life chasing money
Only to end up alone
And broke

My Ship

I am watching and waiting for my ship to come in
I would go out to meet it
But I never learned how to swim
I have finally made my way to the shore
And I am just too tired to move any more
The journey to this point in itself was rough
So I'm just sitting right here because I have had enough
I've done my part in getting here
Yet the way to get to my ship is unclear
That ship holds everything and getting to it is a necessity
The problem is that coming this far
Has taken so much out of me
The road was hard and the trials were great
I wanted to be early but somehow it feels like I'm late
I have worked hard and I have sweated a lot
Yet aches and pains seem to be all that I've got
As I wait here for my ship to come to port
I think about my journey and things of that sort
Like the detour on my way that caused me to slow down
And the fact that I want to swim out to meet it
But I'm afraid that I'd drown
My ship is on the horizon it's close
And yet so far
I have decided not to reflect others
But be my own star
With that decision made
I get up and look for a way
Because if my ship won't come to me then I'm going out to it today

Daddy's Little Girl

Since conception
He's been here
Watched me kick and squirm
Waiting nervously for his turn
To hold me
Wondering about the type of father he'd be
Making plans to protect and provide
For
Even while I was still inside
See
He knew he wanted to give me the world
Long before I was born
I was already Daddy's Little Girl

Late night feedings
Early morning diaper runs
Then came the teething
And all of my number ones
First step
First word
First day of day care
Then the realization that I didn't want to share
My dad with anyone else
As I grew older
We grew closer
Each the apple of the other's eye
Daddy's Little Girl am I

My teen years come and go
A little rebellion disrupts the flow
But onward the river flows
Because I know
That through thick and thin
I can always depend on him
One day he takes my hand
And gives it to the man
With whom I will share my life
And although I am now a wife
I will always be
Daddy's Little Girl

First daughter
Then wife
Now mother
And so many other
Things
Felt both the joy and pain that life brings
Though the rain may fall for a while
There are certain things that can always make me smile
Like watching my daughter play the games I used to play
While hearing my father say the things he used to say
To me
When we played the same games
Yes
She's PawPaw's baby
But I'm still Daddy's Little Girl

He pushed my stroller then balanced my bike
Played chauffer then taught me how to drive
Showed me things I could never learn in school
Like the love of God and the Golden Rule
My first hero
And first love
Father
Friend
All of the above
And so much more
Now it's my turn to care for
You
In your last days
But even after you've left this world
I will still and forever be
Daddy's Little Girl

Flying Solo

Lost in the darkness
Consumed by the pain
What was a light drizzle
Now a category five hurricane
Lightning flashes through his body
Totally unannounced
Peace is desired
If only an ounce
That's the one point he can't seem to score
And even understanding what it's all for
Doesn't make it any easier to bear
Needing
Yet fearing
The ability to share
He refuses to allow his spirit to be crushed
But sometimes the weight is just too much
Too many responsibilities
Desires
Goals
Too many pieces being taken from the whole
Too many matches pretending to be flames
That he'd rather sit in the dark than play those games
Personal pain handled by a solitary mind
Gave new sight to one who was blind
Things once ignored were now seen clear
He could acknowledge
But not release
His fear
Fear and pain

A dangerous combination
Which he used as strength and motivation
He refused to give in
Refused to fall
Every time he stumbled
He'd still stand tall
When true help was offered
He accepted in part
Because accepting in whole
Might've risked his heart
Being skinned alive or gargling with Raid
Was more desirable to him than being betrayed
He had felt that feeling before
Never again
He avoided attachments
No lovers
Few friends
He preferred to make his heart a stone
Than have someone
And still feel alone
Then one night he heard a voice
That caused him to question his choice
Of being the pilot of a single seat plane
Because it drew him out of the darkness
And above the pain

Paper

You can't be me
So why do you try
How 'bout being yourself
Go on
Give it a try
It has to be easier than copying me
Because you can only imitate what you see
You don't know why I do the things that I do
And without that
Your actions could never be true
Besides
You can only fake the funk for so long
Eventually your shot at originality will be gone
You have to learn yourself
And that takes time
You've already wasted most of your life trying to copy mine
Just stop it
Enjoy being you while you still can
Paper was meant to be copied
Not a woman or a man

The Difference

Anger and grief are NOT the same thang
Yet for most of us
They both bring pain
Some get them mixed up and want to lash out
When it might be better to find a way to talk about
What you're feeling
Inside your heart
Because that is normally where grief finds its start
Anger
On the other hand
Starts a little higher
Thinking too much normally stokes that fire
Most men get it twisted
Because
To them
Grief is a woman's emotion
And it's alright for a man to be angry is a popular notion
Now
From that nonsense
Let me give you some relief
Women do get angry
And men can feel grief
Those are human emotions
They don't have a sex or age
We all need to know which one we're feeling
So that we can turn the page
It's easy to get them mixed up because of the pain that you feel
But you have to get them straight
So that you can start to heal

Feeling them both at the same time
Is enough to eat at your heart
And mind
So get it together
So you can tell them apart

Cubic

Supposed to be hard to find
Not able to be bought a dozen to a dime
Work for it
Pay the price
Don't get impatient
Take your time
If it's built too fast
I promise it won't last
The higher the investment
The more precious the jewel
Don't be fooled
By the knockoffs
They look good at first glance
But don't stand a chance
In a light drizzle
Definitely not a storm
You've been warned
Keep off the grass
There are snakes in there
You need to be prepared
Before you take that walk
Do more than talk
Listen
Pay attention
To the things not being said
Or you'll end up out of your head
With worry and wonder
What God put together
No man can put asunder

But was God's hand even in this
Or were you betrayed by the kiss
Of lusts lips
On your tip
Get a grip
And strip
All pretenses away
Before you regret the day
You gave a diamond
To a pretty fake

I Wish

I wish I had a dad that I could miss
That I wanted to see on Father's Day
But if I'm writing this
Then it must not be that way
My father was rarely in my life
Even though my mother was once his wife

I wish that things had been different for them
That they had waited to make me
That before my daddy took that swim
He had thought of how his future would be
But I guess there was a purpose God had a plan
If things had been different I wouldn't be who I am

I wish I could let go of the pain that I feel
From not having my father in my life
I know that I have to be completely healed
Before I can be ready to be a good wife
Because that's just more baggage on an already long list
And even though it hasn't happened yet every day
I wish

Phoenix

Out of the ashes
I rise
Shaking off the dust of deceit and lies
Rising above the hurt and pain
Letting my past fall like rain
During a thunderstorm
My cold heart has now become warm
God has wiped every tear from my eye
But
I am still a little bit gun shy
So
I simply avoid new people
And don't go out with my friends that are single
But I was able to look back on us and simply smile
Which is something that I haven't been able to do for a while
The tears still sometimes flow
And my heart still hurts
But that smile today didn't take so much work
It wasn't forced
It was genuine
Which is the first in a long time
The healing isn't complete
The process isn't through
I've just finally accepted that living is something that I have to do
My life didn't stop at the end of that relationship
I can't imagine
While my life's been on pause
How many blessings I've skipped
Obviously for me to grow

That relationship had to go down in flames
But I know that
Like the phoenix
I shall rise again

Another Man's Wife

You're supposed to be her man but
She won't let you take her on a date
And when you do see her
It's either really early
Or extremely late
She talks about her kids and all the stuff they're into
There've been programs games and concerts
But she's never invited you
The only number you have for her is the cell
Not the job or the house
I hate to tell you this but
That woman is somebody's spouse
Maybe they went before the preacher
Or just a justice of the peace
But that is somebody's wife and your relationship must cease
No matter the excuses
Or how she tries to make it seem right
There is a really good reason that she can never spend the night
And that reason happens to share her address and her last name
You're being played
And it really is a shame
Because this experience is gonna make you bitter
And kind of cold
Simply because the truth is something she never told
She wanted you
But knew you weren't that type of guy
So instead of leaving you alone
She decided to lie
It happens sometimes

This is one of those hard lessons in life
Just try to make sure the next time you get involved
It's not another man's wife

Cougar's Last Dance

Sitting home alone
Feeling kind of down
No reason to go out because the word's gotten around
That you're just out hunting for someone to hurt
There's not a soap known to man that can wash away your dirt
How did I hear about it
Hmmm
Let me see
Somebody told somebody
Who told somebody
Who told me
The stuff I heard had me shaking my head
You left a trail of young bucks wishing they were dead
Or at least a little depressed that you ran out of their life
You didn't bother telling them that you weren't trying to be the wife
Truth be told
You didn't even want to be the girlfriend
And when their feelings were shown
The relationship had to end
Now it's your turn to feel heartache and pain
Because no one wants to lie where so many others have lain
You enjoyed playing that role
About the future you weren't concerned
Your past has caught up with you now
And all your bridges have been burned
One thing you hardly hear about
And the movies rarely show
Is what happens to the cougars when their looks and health just go

When you can no longer rock the heels or drop it like it's hot
When your discount at Denny's and SSI is pretty much all you've got
Somebody should've warned you that the ride had to end
And that when it did
You might want at least one friend
Someone to talk to
Maybe a hand to hold
Who wouldn't mind the fact that you were kind of old
Or maybe someone did try
And you just didn't care
You saw where others ended up
But didn't think you'd go there
While on this road
You threw away chance after chance
Not realizing that you'd soon be dancing
The cougar's last dance

Party Time

It's time to party
Harvest time has come
The trees are ready
Let's have some fun
Choose a spot
Sow your seed
A strong arm is all you need
Don't think too long
Just do the deed
No one will stop you or get in your way
Just pick a spot
You can harvest all day
Tell the band to feel free to play
Add to the festivities of the day
Now
Make sure the branch is good and strong
And your rope
Is nice and long
Make sure the noose is fixed up tight
Gotta get the harvest good and right
You're gonna sleep good tonight
Ignore the sounds on the wind
It's time for the harvest to begin
Deaf ears turned to the begging and pleading
Taking pleasure in the proceedings
Ignoring the trees as they cry and groan
Oblivious to the earth's sighs and moans
Assuming that all are in agreement with you
As you do what you want to

But nature doesn't want any part
Hurt by the blackness of some men's hearts
Rebelling through the branch's sway
Creaking heard right before it gives way
From the weight of the strange fruit
Unable to stop those who shoot
At the ones whose necks don't break
Even animals know it's wrong to take
Something
That you can't give back
For absolutely no reason
It should be considered treason
To the human race
But you equate his value
With the color of his face
The pigment in his skin
Cause you to commit the most atrocious sins
With a smile
Holding the hands of a smiling child
With your family all around
As his blood saturates the ground
His family is scared
Scattered to the wind
But you're dining on lunch while the crows dine on him
Take a picture as a souvenir
Get real close
Make sure it's clear
Chop off the parts that you want to keep
Then start the fire
His rotting flesh is starting to reek
Party time is over

Time to call it a night
You've made your world a little more light
With the darkest actions known to man
Yet you can still kiss your wife and take the preacher's hand
You've convinced yourself that the ones you killed aren't human
but something less than
I guess we'll see what your god says when
Before him you stand

Oasis

When my spirit is in turmoil
He is Neptune calming my seas
When my life is in darkness
He is the sun that shines on me
Even when his own life looks like the coast after a category five
He finds a way to touch that place deep inside
And make me smile
Giving me a feeling that lasts more than a little while
Blessing is too small a word
There is no description that I've ever heard
That can describe perfectly
Exactly what he is to me
My oasis
Cooling water
Relaxing me
When no one else will bother
Or no one else can
Always there with a helping hand
Or soothing voice
In the hurricane
He is my eye
Centering me
Holding my wings
Until I can fly
On my own
Again
More than a friend
Unlableable
No title needed

Before the call was even made
It was heeded
Rescued me from myself
Talks to me like no one else
Took this lonely doll off the shelf
And held her
Warms me when I'm cold
Hearted
Pushes me to finish what I've started
Not demanding
Simply understanding
Exactly what I
Require
When my life is a desert
He
Is the only water that I desire

Butterfly

A butterfly gets its beauty through its struggle
Not even it can avoid trouble
No creature lives inside a bubble

Resistance brings strength
You must fight to survive
If you've never felt pain
Are you really alive

You can't hide in your cocoon
Eventually it'll be too small
Once you've run out of room
You'll fight for freedom with your all

Pain is life
Go ahead and address it
We all misstep
Go ahead and confess it

A phoenix is reborn in the fire
It uses its issues to climb higher
Others can't help but admire

The heat brings out
What's been there all along
Finally you realize
You've always been strong

In the heat of the inferno
There's no need to scream
All you need to know
Is the heat is bringing you closer to your dream

The only time you fail
Is when you choose not to try
It takes darkness and struggle
For the caterpillar to become a butterfly

Small Circle

Some smiles are deceitful
Some words just pretty lies
Some
Claiming to be friends
Are actually just enemies in disguise
It doesn't matter how long someone's been in your life
They may simply stick around to watch your stress and strife
Misery loves company
Just in case you didn't know
This is why
Some people
You should just let go
Stop ignoring the signs that are clear as day
Some people need to be sent on their way
Because this life is hard enough without the added mess
Of people who seem to live off of other's stress
You were meant to stand out
You were meant to shine
Be leery of those who want to douse your light all the time
You may be related to them
Or feel some other sort of obligation
But you still need to cut them loose with no further hesitation
They're not on your side
Not playing for your team
They're living a nightmare
And trying to kill your dream
Giving advice that sounds good at the start
But is meant to leave you with shattered dreams
And a broken heart

Some people are only available to answer your call
In hopes that they will be there to see you fall
Offering hugs so as to easily reach your back
So they can quickly drop you after the attack
It might be time to put your grandmother's records to good use
Remember that smiling faces
Smiling faces
Sometimes
They don't tell the truth
It's better to have a small circle of people who really care
Than to be walking amongst cannibals
Totally unaware
It's not your flesh
But your soul they want to devour
Because from dream crushing is where they get their power
Take the time in your life to do some calculations
And subtract the ones around whom trouble seems to be in constant multiplication
Those who divide your blessings without adding a thing
Erase them from your life before any more issues they bring
You don't need to claim a lot of friends
Life isn't a popularity contest
Get rid of the emotional leeches
So in peace
You can rest
You'll be less anxious
Your life will feel more worthwhile
If you simply shake off those snakes with deceitful smiles

Diamonds

A diamond has to be cut to shine
That's what I was told by a friend of mine
A lot of stress and pressure is what it takes
To distinguish a real diamond
From the fakes
But the problem in this world today
Is that most folks don't want it that way
They want the fakers
Fronters
And clones
Just so that they don't feel alone
They don't know themselves
So they don't care to know you
As long as you do what others expect you to
Act like this
Dress like that
Your head is only for holding a hat
You see
There's so much following going on
That individuals are viewed as wrong
The diamonds in this world are treated like trash
Because the world no longer values class
That doesn't make the diamonds' value any less
Although it does cause a certain feeling of hopelessness
The diamond will shine brighter once it's been cut
Yes it's a painful process
Just don't give up

The Things They Carried

He carried the world on his shoulders and his past on his back
No one could see his burden so they couldn't take up the slack
Some wouldn't have wanted to even if they could
They preferred adding to the weight and that was no good

She carried her children's future and her mother's dreams
Gave away parts of herself that could never be redeemed
Just to be a good mother and good daughter
Trying to replace the irreplaceable a son and a father

He carried the goals and dreams of himself and future generations
Yet he seemed to feel he'd never actually reach his destination
Too many detours potholes and breakdowns
Sometimes it seemed easier to just give up and lie down

She carried bruises and scars heavily veiled
The narrator of her life was writing a very painful tale
Heartbreak and loss thoughts of suicide
Memories of days she lived when she would've gladly died

He carried alone a weight that should have been shared
It's not that no one else knew just that no one else cared
The weight of his ancestors and descendants unborn
No way to please either yet the desire to kept him torn

She carried secrets that she just couldn't release
Even though letting them go would have given her such peace
These secrets were the mortar in her wall
And she just refused to even think about letting it fall

He carried a desire to feel love and devotion
Instead he got madness drama and constant commotion
Didn't want to fight but had no choice
Had to scream or they would ignore his voice

She carried a need to be protected
Instead she was constantly rejected
She didn't meet their standards hers were too high
Many nights she slept alone on a pillow whose case was not dry

He carried the key and the wrecking ball
To unlock her heart and knock down her walls
But under all his mess they were hidden away
And he had no intention of them ever seeing the light of day

She carried the peace that he longed for
And the longing to be so much more
Than just some man's late night hype
But she didn't think she was his type

They were made for each other
Their time had come
Destined to be lovers
Yet prepared to run
At the first sign of anything hard
Both refusing to let down their guard
They couldn't help the attraction
The connection was there
They guarded their actions
And were totally aware

Of the feelings the other attempted to hide
Both claiming to have given up on love knowing they'd lied

Loads were shared
Secret scars bared
As natural as the next breath
Connections accepted
Ideas respected
Between them no secret kept
Less anger
Less tears
Less complaints
Less fears
Smiles increased
Negativity released
Realized this was the one for whom they should've tarried
Freed each other from the weight of the things they carried

Copycats

A copycat can never be the original
No matter how hard they try
There will always be *something* that gives away their lie
No matter what they do
No matter what they say
They can't be someone else
No how
No way
They may walk the same or wear clothes of the same sort
But when it comes to being the original
They always fall short
There are copycats all over the world
All sizes and races
Man
Woman
Boy and girl
Chances are you know one
Maybe two or three
Unless of course you're one
Because it's definitely not me
Copycats
At some point
Bought into the story
That the only way to shine
Is to steal someone else's glory
Their own light is dim or turned off
Possibly unplugged
But
For whatever reason

They're lost
They've lost who they are and the dreams that they had
So they imitate others and it's really quite sad
Because they have so much to offer
So much to give
If
Instead of someone else's
Their own life they'd live
But they don't know how
Maybe they never learned
Or something major happened and
From their own path
They turned
There is one thing about this life that I definitely know
There will be rough spots no matter which way you go
And if you don't know who you are
It'll be even harder at that
Life is hard enough
Without being a copycat

Skewed

Excuse me
I'm sorry
I don't mean to be rude
But our justice system is terribly skewed
Beyond a shadow of a doubt
That's what they say
But if your skin is shadowed
Then on that bed you **will** lay
It's legalized lynching down in the south
Not as quick for some
But they're still taking us out
Acquitted for our beatings murders and rapes
It seems from this nightmare
We just can't seem to escape
If this is the land of the brave and the home of the free
Then why are there some who are still trying to enslave me
Pedophiles go free in spite of boatloads of proof
Yet minority males are locked up in their youth
For petty crimes committed
Or worse
Ones that weren't
We're not so far removed from the days when crosses were being burnt
In someone's front yard
As a way to keep us in check
Then they wonder why some have no respect
They say their intentions are simply being misconstrued
But I still say that the justice system is terribly skewed

Stop the Madness

You'll say and do practically anything to get his attention
Ignoring the fact that he makes it a point to constantly mention
His girl
You know
The lady in his life
The one that he says he wants to make his wife
And yet
You refuse to back down
Offering your company whenever his woman is out of town
Do you really think so badly of yourself
That you would take the scraps from someone else
It wouldn't be so bad if you were the only one
But
Everywhere I look I see this being done
Women chasing men that are already attached
Men chasing women that have already found their match
Who's really to blame in this situation
Who's the actual cause of all this aggravation
The one doing the chasing
Or the one being chased
Would the chaser keep chasing if more opposition was faced
If the chasee wasn't so charming
Would the chaser still care
Or are they more turned on when the other acts unaware
This is a worldwide epidemic
And it really needs to stop
If everyone had their own
Then maybe the divorce rate would drop
Instead

The women look desperate
And the men look they have fleas
If there's a way to stop the madness
I wish somebody would tell me please

What If?

Whether mother
Father
Lover
Or friend
We always wonder
When a life comes to an abrupt end
What if I had said this
Or done that
Unanswered questions keep you looking back
And the imagination that you thought was long gone
Suddenly wakes up and is Superman strong

What if I hadn't done that or said this
Should I have given them one more hug or kiss
You can't change what happened
It can't be undone
And stressing yourself sick
Really helps no one
\
What if it had been me
Is a question we love to ask
God obviously has more for you to do and they have completed their task
Accidents happen
That's just a part of life
But the damage they cause
Can cut like a knife

What if I had been there
Would it still be the same
Or am I just making it harder on myself
Playing the "what if" game
You will one day get to a place where you can look back and smile
The tears will still come
But only once in a while
You'll be able to see them as one of God's greatest gifts
And you'll no longer ask yourself
What if

You Say

You say you're always thinking about me
That I'm priority one
But I get the leftovers when everything else is done
Finances
Family
And even football
Are more important to you
Yet you throw a fit whenever you start to feel like number two
I have been more patient than I would ever have thought
If love is a trap
Then I have been thoroughly caught
And I want out
'Cause I don't like all these tears
Somebody needs to rescue me
Or I'm gonna be stuck for years
But maybe I deserve this for all the dirt I've done
If I'm reaping what I've sown
When will the harvest be done
If this is how I've ever caused someone else to feel
Then from this day forward
I promise to keep it real
I may hurt your feelings
You may not like what you hear from me
But I don't ever want to hold someone back
Who'd do better free
I hear what you're telling me but I don't see it that way
Actions speak louder than words
And that drowns out what you say

Remember Me

I am the soldier that never came home
I stepped on a mine and my body parts went to spots unknown
Remember me

I am the soldier that that black flag flies for
I am either missing in action or a prisoner of war
Remember me

I am the soldier that came back but my mind was not whole
Now they want to call my crazy but this wasn't my goal
Remember me

I am the soldier whose spouse cheated on me while I was risking my life
No enemy can ever cause as much pain as an unfaithful husband or wife
Remember me

I am the soldier who still has the heart to fight but is no longer physically able
They forced me to come home I couldn't even take my brothers' meals to the table
Remember me

I am the soldier that chose no prosthetic 'cause I wanted you to see
Exactly what I gave for my country
Remember me

I am the soldier whose children follow them from base to base
They learned young to not get attached to any one place
Remember me

I am the soldier who was used for my benefits
I wanted a soul mate they wanted what they could get
Remember me

I am the soldier who took the blame I took the fall
Even though it was my commanding officer that made the call
Remember me

I am the soldier that shows my love for this country in the most sacrificial way
Yet most people don't even think about me on Memorial Day
Remember me

Fake

You know you faker than a three dollar bill
Right
Saying you won't when we all know you will
Matter of fact
You already have
You still claimin' to be real
Don't make me laugh
You haven't been real since yo' daddy squirted you out
Cuz he was thinkin' he'd rather have had the mouth
Nine months later
You arrived with a scream
Yo' momma wishin' it was all a bad dream
Daddy was long gone
He had ran out of lies
And you look just like him
'Specially round the eyes
Ya momma pretended to love you 'til you were old enough to tell
Then you pretended home was heaven
Knowing it was hell
You pretendin'
She pretendin'
And then before long
You looked around and realized that yo' childhood was gone
And now that you're on your own
And outta that house
You pretend to be a man
When you're really a mouse
Sellin' drugs
Tatted up

Packin' heat
Doin' what it takes to get cred in the streets
I'm just keepin' it real
Is yo' constant excuse
Knowin' you just as fake as one percent juice
At least you know what a condom is
So no babies will you make
That's one less generation that'll grow up fake

Dark Night

She wanted to go with big brother
We saw no harm
Such a sweet little lady
So full of charm
Never mean
A smile for everyone
Her life was ended by a nut with a gun
This wasn't a drive by
No stray bullet on the block
Not that those things are right
But when will the madness stop
Is there no place safe for our children anymore
Or should we keep them inside behind a bullet proof door
That won't save my baby
She's lost to me
Just because the movies
Is where she wanted to be
At first you had to worry about gangs
Or someone on drugs
Now it's the clean cut kid who could never be a thug
Was he mistreated as a child
Was there no love in his home
Was he given too much attention
Or constantly left alone
These questions and more are quickly driving me insane
He'll be famous forever while they'll soon forget my child's name
She's just one of many on a long list of injured or dead
I keep imagining her pain and fear
Somebody please get this out of my head

I don't want to go on without her
That just doesn't seem right
I'm just going through the motions
'Cause my life ended
On that dark night

The Story

There once was a man
From a different time
Who lived in a fantasy land that he had created in his mind
In this world
His opinions were always right
And no one around him ever had a fight
He had no secrets
There was no pain in his past
The problem with the fantasy was that it couldn't last
One day something happened that was really quite strange
He met someone that made him want to change
To grow up
And let go of his fantasy
But a way out
He really couldn't see
So instead
He tried to find a way to let her in
As far as he was concerned
That way was a win-win
The problem was
She had been too long in the real world
So she wanted him to come out so that she could be his girl
For them to be together there just didn't seem to be a way
But he was determined to have her
And she was determined to stay
He wanted to have her even if letting go of his fantasy was the cost
She was willing to go in and get him
Even if she might get lost

His emergence was like birth and caused just as much pleasure and pain
They both knew that to get to the sunshine
They had to go through the rain
Some days were hard and into his fantasy he would retreat
These days made her want to give up but she refused to be beat
She hated the ones that had hurt him and made him build those walls
Especially since he still ran to them every time that they called
His family was the reason that he was less than whole
But he had never been complete so he didn't know how to make that his goal
There were some walls inside him that had been up for so long
That
According to him
That was exactly where they belonged
Whenever she got close to those walls
The fights were fierce
They would say and do things to cause the other's heart to feel pierced
Or maybe crushed
But definitely in some way broke
These were the times when some very mean and hateful words were spoke
By him
Because he was afraid of what she might learn
And by her
Because she had decided that his walls needed to burn
Because what he viewed as safe and secure
She saw as a disease with a very complex cure
He'd lived in his fantasy world for so long

It seemed that
What she called reality
Was really the dream
And a painful one
So he wanted no part of that
He'd always ran from pain
That's how he was taught to act
She made him confront it
Which was something that he'd never tried
But his walls took up too much space
So they had to come down if she was to get inside
The problem she faced
From one day to the next
Was that he was building new walls faster than the old ones
She could wreck
There were times when she felt like just giving in
That this was a battle that she could never win
But she had seen a glimpse of the man trapped behind those walls
And that gave her the strength to do her best to make them fall
When she saw that he had help making sure that those walls were strong
She knew that
Without him
She wouldn't be able to fight for long
One day it happened
She just gave up and sat down
He peeked out over the wall because he heard a terrible sound
The sound was her crying and admitting defeat
She was completely drained and had been thoroughly beat
Now it was all on him
He had to make a choice

He could go out and console her
Or
Stay in and ignore her voice
He took so long to decide that those who were keeping him started to worry
I don't know what happened next because he has yet to write the rest of the story

Reflection

The water is cold and my reflection is clear
I sit on the bank
Wondering how I got here
Out in the wilderness
Cold and alone
Facing a pain that I have never known
As I gaze into the eyes looking up at me
There are so many things that I don't want to see
Pain and bitterness
Heartache and regret
And a lot of other stuff that I'd rather forget
Looking at my reflection I can see all that in my eyes
Eyes are the window to the soul
So I know they can't lie
I wait for a flood to wash away both me and my reflection
And take my life in a new direction
One that will help me forget this pain and heartache
That will allow the tears to dry up that formed this lake
As I stare at my reflection
The ripples begin
And I realize that I am crying
Yet again
I want to get up and leave this place
To go where I can see a reflection of a happier face
But I don't know how I got here or where I'm at
So how am I supposed to find my way back
I need a guide
Someone to lead the way
To a place where there's the chance of a brighter day

I can't get away
Not on my own
My tears washed away the path and this lake has grown
I never knew it was possible to feel so much pain
Or that your eyes could be the clouds and your tears the rain
I vaguely remember a time when I was someone somewhere else
But now I just sit here
A reflection of my former self

Seed

Be careful my sons
there's something you don't seem to understand
The seed is the most important thing when it comes to populating the land
A forest can be burned and grow back as good as new
Because the seed was protected
that's why I'm trying to protect you
Your seed is your power
don't just give it away
Look at the land you're fertilizing
is that really where you want to stay
The land that you fertilize should be a choice selection
Or your seed may grow to hate you
that's just the natural progression
And don't ever force your seed into unwilling ground
The resulting growth is apt to bring you down
You come from the seed of kings
and that's what you carry
So your seed should only be shared with the queen that you marry
Stop falling for the lie that your seed should be planted anywhere
That's just a trick
because you lose your power the more that you share
When seed is watered down and planted in ground that is not right
For something good to grow
It takes even more effort
nourishment
and light
So before you plant a seed
make sure you're ready to give it some time and dedication

That will cut down on so much pain
confusion
and aggravation
The desire to groom your seed and watch it grow should outweigh
every other need
In it is your very essence
so please
protect your seed

Reap

I got him I got him I finally got him
She went a little crazy and actually shot him
But he survived and she went to jail
She keeps saying that it's my fault that her life went to hell
I had to have him from the moment that our eyes met
He wasn't being satisfied was my bet
And I must've been right because now he's with me
I'll be the woman that she couldn't be
Somebody said that what goes around comes around but I don't care
He's mine now and I know that he'll always be there

It's been years since I took him I almost forgot
Until I woke up to find that another woman had my spot
Not with him because he left me a long time ago
Once the newness wore off he was out the do'
I felt so stupid but it was a lesson learned
I never thought that one day it would be my turn
Now I know how she felt and why she did what she did
I thought that she was the immature one now I see that I was the kid
Thinking that I could wreck someone's relationship and get away clean
Now here I am being replaced by a girl who's nineteen

What was I thinking leaving my lady for this chick
I threw away a diamond 'cause I was thinking with my dick
She fought for me and I just laughed
I didn't realize then what I had
I acted like she was crazy and I was justified
Now I want to fix this but can't get past my pride
She's still single but colder than ice
She took me back once but I doubt she'll do it twice
And I don't blame her I'd do the same in her shoes
So I just sit here drinking listening to the blues

They didn't last and I'm not surprised
While I served my time I realized
That he wasn't ready he didn't deserve me
But since I've gotten out I'm really lonely
I've wanted to reach out to him but can't get past this wall
My pain and pride say No every time I want to call
I don't date at all because I'm so afraid
To open myself up again and then get played
I'm not able to love simply because I can't trust
He took that away from me when he gave in to his lust

He was the one obligated so he was the one that was wrong
But when someone is persistent you can only resist for so long
Maybe no one ever told her to not chase another woman's man
Or maybe karma is something that she just didn't understand
I heard that she got married to a guy from her youth
But after a few years she learned a hard truth
There's always someone that wants what you have
Always someone that at your pain they'll laugh
She woke up one morning and heard my voice from long ago
Saying Remember baby girl you reap what you sow

Police State

This is supposed to be America
Home of the free
Land of the great
Yet it's becoming more and more like a police state
The biggest gangs wear uniforms and get regular paychecks
They beat people down
Sell drugs and sex
We're expected to bow down just because of who they are
Stand idly by while they ransack our car
They get commended for things that would put a civilian in jail
And sadly
This madness is going on on a worldwide scale
Now there may be some good guys in law enforcement
Don't get me wrong
But the bad ones have been in power for way too long
So the good guys need to do a better job
Because of the ones that act like the police force is the mob
It's not just the cops
It's the politicians too
Who feel like they don't have to follow the same rules that the rest of us do
This is a major threat to the life of this nation
We give up more and more freedoms with each generation
We've become so lazy that we don't even care
That the things that we want for our grandchildren might not be there
Our safety and freedom is an illusion at best
And we keep losing more every time we fail a test
The test of what we value
What's priority one
We've sacrificed our future for a little bit of fun
We're supposedly a progressive nation
But I wonder what's our goal
What does it profit a man to gain the world and lose his soul
Or maybe that's the problem
we don't care about that stuff
We've been convinced that living this life is more than enough

That death is the end and Heaven just a myth
Our freedoms are disappearing faster than a fifth
Of gin
At the bar that all the cops drink at
While they're laughing about the crimes they committed to make their pockets fat
And complain about the politicians that are even more crooked than they are
I feel sorry for the good guys
I know they won't get far
Not unless they compromise their morals and give up peaceful sleep
Because once they bend that first rule
They're already in too deep
That will be used against them to get them to do more and more
Then the choice becomes continue
Or be afraid to open your door
As citizens it's our fault that this stuff is allowed
There was a time we should have stood
But instead we bowed
If we don't come together before it's too late
We'll wake up one morning living in a police state

Name

I can be anything online
It's my choice
You don't have to see my face
Or hear my voice
I can be sexy and smart
The flyest around
A virtual genius
Always laying knowledge down
It doesn't matter that these pics are ten years old
Or that the hot sexy smile has long since been cold
All that matters are the comments and the attention
Not my spouse and kids that I forgot to mention
I'm just a con man with an image to sell
It's not my fault if you get caught up in the lies that I tell
When I came knocking
You gladly opened the door
Not understanding what I was really there for
I'm not in your life to lift you up or improve
I simply enjoy playing head games and have a point to prove
We'll never meet up
You'll never see my face
I just want to know that I can control that space
In between your ears where your brain is supposed to be
I want to be your god
I want you to worship me
I want to be able to control when you smile and when you cry
Before you come to your senses
You'll love the way I lie
One day you'll move on
You'll get tired of my game
But you won't even know who to be mad at 'cause I never told you my real name

The Secret

He hurt me
and it was the most unbearable pain
The physical has passed
and I've hidden the shame
But the pain she caused
far outweighed his
Because when she found out
she just covered up what he did
I was innocent and she should have been my protection
Instead
pleasing him was her immediate selection
Yet I still showed her love
and held the secret in
growing colder daily
hating him
And that hate consumed me for so long
That at the first chance for freedom
I was gone
But
a piece of me was left at that house
A piece I was too ashamed to share with my spouse
The secret ate at me
and daily I died
Wanting to let go
but holding it all inside
I was used to it by then
you have to understand
The secret was held in a death grip in my mind's hands
I wanted to tell the world
shout it from the rooftops
But every time I started to
that mental muzzle made me stop
And decades later
I still nurse that pain within my self
Having to deal with my child saying "momma" to someone else
My child knows who I am
through an overheard fight

From the pain that was caused
I could have died that night
I had to relive the conception
and all the other abuse
And for keeping that secret
I realized there was no excuse
I had done no wrong
this mess was not my fault
I was only a child
I couldn't have stopped the assault
The two who were responsible had gotten off scot-free
Because I figured out too late that no one would blame me
Except for one who doesn't seem to understand
That I was just a child
I didn't seduce that man
I couldn't argue about how things were done
And I couldn't leave
there was no place to run
Now a new generation is here
that doesn't know the truth
The lies that were planted are now bearing fruit
Fruits of more pain
distrust
and insecurities
All because my mother chose him
over me

Lonely Road

One day
When I'm old and gray
A man will come along
Look at me and say
I know that you're afraid and I understand
But it's almost over
Please take my hand
I gave up on love just like you
So I know exactly what you've been going through
Faking a smile for all of your friends
Wondering if and when the pain will end
Hating the loneliness but afraid of the pain
Avoiding the sunshine for fear of the rain
You could write a book full of the excuses you've used over the years
To cover up your doubts and justify your fears
I could be your co-author because I've walked the same path
My life was full of subtractions and I got tired of the math
So I divided myself between work and home
Became a hermit and stayed alone
But that life has gotten old and so have I
I'd like to know a little love before I die
Just a little peace amidst all of the stress and strife
So if it's not too much trouble
Would you be my wife

Alive

Some things in life will never change
No matter how much of your life you rearrange
We all know this and yet we continue
Going through the same stuff that we've already been through
Because we fool ourselves into thinking that this time won't be the same
That we're suddenly going to win even though we've constantly lost this game
Maybe we are all crazy maybe that's it
Just a bunch of unconfessed gluttons for punishment
Or maybe
Just maybe
It's something else
Something we can't even define ourselves
Something deep inside that won't let us give up
That makes us keep revving that mental engine even though we're stuck
We all want to believe that there is some purpose to this life
That there is a reason for all the pain heartache stress and strife
I guess it's simply human nature at its core
To get knocked down and still get up for more
We take the bumps and bruises and all of the scars
Then get back up and reach for the stars
Or our dreams whatever they may be
Because whenever we close our eyes that's all we see
So we can't give up on our dreams we have to push toward our goals
That's the only way to quench the fire that burns in our souls
Though it hurts some times and we may shed a few tears
We continue pressing on in spite of our fears
Because if we gave up or gave in we'd never be satisfied
It's through the pain and struggle that we know we're still alive

Whipped

Why is it when a man is faithful
He's gotta be whipped
Who exactly wrote that line into the script
Why is it ok for men to sleep around
If a woman tried that
Her name would be run into the ground
And what about those women that encourage men to cheat
I think they should all be taken out into a field and beat
Yeah I know
The ultimate choice is his
But these chicks know how to exploit relational weaknesses
They bring him lunch when wifey's too busy at work
They stroke his ego
Build him up when he's hurt
But what they don't get
Is all they'll ever be is a chick on the side
Because there is a reason that he made the other woman his bride
And for the few that actually do get the man
There's something that they just don't seem to understand
The same thing that he did to her
He'll probably do to you
Then you'll be all alone and what will you do
You'll probably look for the kind of guy that you talked about
The one who loved his woman enough to ignore you when your cheeks were hanging out
Only problem is
The reputation that you've earned
You're going to have to prove that
From your old ways
You have turned
Which may take more time than you have
Or are willing to spend
So here's a little advice
Before on your journey you begin
Instead of chasing after a faithful man that's feeling a little neglected
How 'bout you meet some single guys

That way you'll be more respected
Or
You can keep talking about how so and so has her man in check
Although they both seem to be happy
While you're a lonely wreck
You'll never have what they have until you start following God's
Holy script
You see
He's faithful because the Spirit
Not his wife
Has him whipped

Lies

I am amazed at how some choose to justify
Instead of just apologize
When caught in a lie
And this is not directed strictly at the men
I've been lied to by
Lovers
Strangers
And friends
At least that's what I thought they were
Until the truth came out
And found that they didn't know what friendship was really about
Don't tell me you love me
Yet can lie to me with ease
Since I'm real with you
Be the same with me please
You've lied so much that it's hard to believe you
I had to go outside and check when you said the sky was blue
Because everything else that you've said has been pure fabrication
So
As far as I'm concerned
You're just a figment of my imagination
There's no way that you can be real and lie all the time like that
Unless you have no heart
Or don't know where your conscience is at
A house of cards is more solid than the words that you say
I'd put more faith in a snow man
Being built in Texas
In May
Than any of the words that come out of your mouth
It's easier to believe that racism is dead in the South
That's just how much my faith in you has been shaken
Due to all the bullshit from you that I've taken
But the thing that still amazes me the most
Is how
Instead of coming clean
You'd rather catch ghost
Just up and disappear when the truth is in your face

As if you
And the truth
Can't be in the same place
Even after I've shot down all of your alibis
You choose to hold tightly to your collection of lies
These lies are important to you
That is so plain to see
I wish you and your lies all the best
Have fun without me

Fool

It's been a while since I've been to school
So I'd like to know
Who's the bigger fool
The one who's taken him back after he's done wrong
Or the one who knows that he's changed
But still tells him to move on
See
I'm in a place where I am thoroughly confused
My heart has been broken
My soul is battered and bruised
Yet I still love him
Is that so wrong
Does pushing him away really make me strong
Or is holding on what's making me weak
Does anyone have the answers that I seek
How many people are miserable because they couldn't forgive
Because
With anger and grudges they chose to live
If he's learned his lesson
If he's really changed
Why does my life have to be rearranged
Why do we have to give up if this is our heart's desire
Maybe these issues were just the refining fire
Meant to show us what really mattered
That our love was too strong to simply be shattered
But my pride keeps me quiet
And I think that his does too
Somebody please tell me what should I do
Give in to my pride
Hold on to this pain
Give up my chance at sunshine
And hide in the rain
Or am I just fooling myself thinking that he wants me back
Is this just a fantasy created to cover the confidence that I lack
I'm hurt and confused because there is no set rule
It seems that either way I'll look like a fool

Tears

I had forgotten how to cry
I hadn't done it in so long
And I have gotten weak
From being so strong
But now it's too much
And I can't seem to stop the flow
I don't have the strength
I've lost my get up and go
The one who built me up has decided to tear me down
So the drought was ended by my tears saturating the ground
I didn't realize that there was so much liquid in me
These tears I'm crying could create a new sea
They just won't stop flowing
Somebody opened the flood gate
This stuff needs to stop before it's too late
Because I'm losing myself with each tear I cry
I need to stop before my soul runs dry
Tears are supposed to be cleansing
But I feel dirtier than ever
I want to turn them off but I can't find the lever
I admit it's my fault
I got in too deep
When I'm not crying
All I want to do is sleep
I'm just going through the motions
A shadow of myself
Praying that there's no more
'Cause I can't take anything else
This is the most pain that I have ever felt in all of my years
I hope this flood will stop before I'm washed away by my tears

Cavemen

Cavemen still exist today
I've dated quite a few
They love to tell their women what they can and cannot do
They don't live in caves
It's an apartment or townhome
Rolling Escalades or convertibles whenever they roam
They want to keep a harem
Like the days of old
And get mad when their women don't do what they're told
Double standards
To them
Is just a way of life
They expect complete faithfulness from their girlfriend
Mistress
And wife
You are never to question a caveman's motives or his moves
And definitely never rebuke him or try to stop his groove
He is
The Man
And you were made to please him
All those women on the side
Just pretend that you don't know about them
That's just how it is
You must follow his rules
And ignore everybody that calls you a fool
You'd rather be with someone that pulls your hair instead of holding your hand
Why be in a real relationship when you can date a caveman

Drinking Sand

All I heard was

I know more than you
About everything
I'm the reason why the birds sing
The sun shines
Whenever I smile
Male models copy my style
When they hit the runway
So I don't see how you can say
That you don't want me
Even a blind woman could see
How hot I am

At this point
My mind goes blank
And he starts to sound
Like Charlie Brown's teacher
Or maybe a drunk preacher
He can keep the collection plate
As I throw one finger in the air
And look for a quick escape
All I did was sneak a glance
Now he thinks I want romance
Couldn't even speak
Before he overpowered me
With his nonsense
What part of the game is this
When an innocent look
Can be mistook
For heated desire
Followed by offers
To put out a fire
That hasn't even started
Common sense has obviously departed
Crushed by his ego
But hey

You know
This was the first
Time
In my life
I saw someone drown
In their own thirst

Side Piece

Yes
They're having troubles
But she still has his heart
The best that you can hope for
Is simply a part
Not of his heart
But of his anatomy
He'll gladly use you to set his body free
And while you're getting caught up
Because he made you shout
He's steadily talking to his woman
Trying to work things out
What is wrong with you woman
Have some pride
Aren't you worth more than just a quick ride
If he'll cheat with you
He'll cheat on you
More often than not
So why are you chasing a man that another woman's already got
Are there no single men available where you live
Or is it that you don't really want to give
Any real time and effort
To a relationship
You'd rather have the leftovers
Just take what you can get
I'm sorry
But I love me more than that
I refuse to be the backup chick for any cat
No matter how charming and attractive he may be
Because no one is going to love me
As much as me
But you go ahead and keep chasing him like you're a dog
He just may take the time to split your forest with his log
Then it's back to his main chick for some major making up
And he won't even be worried about your sorry but
Because he never really cared for you
You were just a distraction

He forgot about you five seconds after getting his sexual satisfaction
See
You taught him how to treat you with you relentless chase
Love and respect aren't what he thinks about when he sees your face
He might think about how wet you get
Or the sounds that you make
But
Home to meet his momma is someplace that he'll never take
You
That's not what he wants you for
You're just a skeleton in his closet
And he's already closed the door
You never had his heart
He just needed a little release
Your push to be the main chick
Only made you
The side piece

Please

Please don't shoot me I've done nothing wrong
I'm only going home I'll be there before long
I'm not a crack head murderer or thief
So please tell me why are you giving me this grief
Yes I'm darker than you but I can't help that
It's just how God made me I was born black
That doesn't make us different our hearts beat the same
How can you hate me and you don't even know my name
If you do this you will make both our families cry
Please don't hurt me I'm too young to die

My family will cry for the loss of life and the separation
But yours will cry for the destruction of their previous reputation
Because who wants to be related to someone who stands accused
Of being a racist murderer whose imagined powers were abused
If you do this your family will be the next internet trend
And will quickly lose respect support and friends
People will look at your brothers as if they had pulled the trigger
And men will stop wanting your sister regardless of her fine figure
Think of your mother if you don't want to think of mine
Please don't kill me you don't want to do time

Or maybe you hate your family just as much as you hate me
Maybe you want to add to their lives pain and misery
Because you're bigger than me and you have a gun
I know I can't win a fight and there's nowhere to run
No one will believe all the lies that you'll tell
Because all around here people heard me yell
And screaming begging for my life
You can't claim self-defense I don't even have a knife
I know that you're not listening my blackness is all you can see
You better pray that God listens when you stand before Him and say please

I Know

Momma I love you
Momma don't cry
I know that it hurt you that I had to die
I can't say I miss you
We don't do that up here
There is no worry
Pain
Sorrow
Or fear
I will be happy on the day that you join me
But until then
Be strong
And try to be happy
I know that there'll be times when you miss me so much
When you would give anything for just one more touch
Please remember that I'm with you
Only my body is missing
You can hear me say Momma I love you
If
With your heart
You'll listen
I know that you miss me
But I live on in you
And living is something that you have to continue to do
Even when it's painful
Even when it's hard
You can't give in
I'll be your guiding star
I'll be that strength you find deep down inside
Momma I love you
Momma don't cry

I Need a Man

I talked to a woman who was with a sorry dude
I tried to wake her up without being rude
Told her that if he really cared
He wouldn't act that way
And in response
This is what she had to say

I need a man
I need a man
Y'all just don't understand
I just cannot be alone
I need a reason to make this house a home
Somebody told me that I was putting a man in a place that only
God can fill
But I aint never met God so
I guess I will
Continue doing
Whatever it takes
To make sure there's a man beside me at night to make me shake
If he wants all my money to stay around
Then I'll get two jobs to hold him down
If his friend is over and he wants to watch me give him head
Then on my knees I'll go
'Cause without him I'd feel dead
My family thinks I'm crazy
And I don't have any friends
I got tired of catching him with them when I came in
Now it's just me and my man
And my kids too
I let him do with them what he wants to do
They say that it hurts but I know that that's a lie
Because he makes me feel good every time he walks by
Sometimes I get mad over the attention that they get
I know my daughter wants him but I can't put her out yet
She's only ten but already a whore
Been taking his time from me since she was four

Sometimes I wonder what the preacher meant when he said that this wasn't God's plan
But then I think about having to be alone and remember that
I need a man

I tried to tell her that Jesus was the lover of her soul
But she was thoroughly convinced that she needed a man to make her whole
I stopped trying to talk to her
There was nothing left to say
I had to put her in God's hands and just continue to pray

The Greatest Commandment

They say we were made in God's image
Yet I can't find any positive images
Of us
Makes me wanna cuss
Or curse
Them
Like He did in the Old Testament
How you gone say you love God
But hate your fellow man
I just don't understand
Show me in the Book
Where it says our love should be based on looks
I don't remember that verse
And what's worse
Is you condemn the next man's religion for hatred and violence
But when your people do it
Straight silence
Since your god allows you to hate
I guess hypocrisy is cool too
Right
You have no trouble sleeping at night
As people who don't look like you
Are battered and bruised
Murdered and misused
By men who
Might be your kin
Or a favorite friend
Y'all might even barbecue together
Take a pic
Make a postcard
Whatever
But
Your god is one of love and peace
Right
I guess
If you say so
All I know

Is that you can stand
With blood on your hands
And worship with a smile
After someone's lost a child
Friend
Spouse
Job
House
Oh Pharisee
Woe to thee
Because love and hate
Can't live in the same place
So if your god does exist
He's gonna be pissed
That you used him as an excuse
To break all of his rules

Charm

Some men love drama
They just won't admit it
They think something is wrong if they have peace for even one minute
They find the craziest women to flirt with
Even though they're taken
Then wanna act surprised when they come home to find the chick in the kitchen
Naked
Bakin'
Pretending to be innocent when they knew all along that the stalker gene
In her
Was strong
Now they're looking at their girl all confused
Trying to explain why they're all battered and bruised
The reason is simple
Although he'll never say
That he thought that he could just do his thing and slip away
Flirt with her a little bit
Inflate his already huge ego
Complain about his girl
And just put on a show
But when he caught ol' girl in his house
That's when stuff got real
She was professing her love and saying she knew he had to feel the same way too
Because of all the laughs they'd shared
All the little things that showed that he cared
When he started laughing
And said girl please
She started crying
And fell to her knees
First she tried begging
Then she offered head
Listing all the things that she could do
In

And out of bed
He kept laughing and said
My girl handles all of that and more
Now you can get up and make your way out of my door
She stood up
But she had come to stay
She told him
With people's emotions
You really shouldn't play
He kept laughing
After all he was the man
He almost saw too late the gun in her hand
She didn't shoot him
But she hit him just right
And she continued hitting him even after she'd put out his lights
Yes this is fiction
But it can easily be real life
And the gun could easily be a car
Bat
Or knife
Wake up and heed this warning
I'm ringing the alarm
Fellas
You need to think twice before you decide to turn on the charm

Sweep

They tell me to sweep around my own front door
But as soon as it's clean
They just throw more
I try to take care of my kids and teach them what's right
But
How do you explain to a child
That they'll always have to fight
Small-minded people
Who have no clue
About the things that they've seen
Or gone through
They say
Why do you rally when your people are done wrong
We've done no worse to you
Than what's been done by your own
There's one concept of war that seems to have been overlooked
If you plan to keep on eating
You have to protect the cook
Still confused
Well
Let me break it down
It's hard to tend to the wounded with bombs crashing all around
These interior struggles
Were caused by exterior pressure
That creates a hopelessness that no man can measure
I tell them
Your people weren't bought and sold
They didn't have to work until they were too old
They say
That stuff is over
Just let it go
I say
It still happens
In case you didn't know
Our sons are oppressed
Our daughters abused
And

About the cause of their pain
They are so confused
So they lash out at those closest at hand
I don't condone it
But I do understand
Whips and chains have been replaced by the media
Laws
And drugs
Modern day slaves are crackheads
Hood rats
Pimps
And thugs
What most call black on black crime
I call the fulfillment of prophecy
A prophecy that was written by our late Uncle Willie
You know him
The one who gave lynching its name
They may not live on plantations
But the concept is the same
Hate your brothers and sisters
Even though they're in the same place
And always remember that you're a part of an inferior race
Those lessons are taught everywhere
From the media to the schools
Then people have the nerve to ask why they act such fools
Generations of self-hatred won't just up and go away
To be deprogrammed
Will take more than a day
We know we have issues
That's what we write for
So before you point them out
Why don't you sweep around your own front door

Contradictions

I am a vegetarian because killing innocent animals is wrong
But I support abortion
You can kill babies all day long
I support religious freedom
They're basically all the same
But I get offended when I hear people pray in Jesus' name
I say the country that I came from is the best that there is
But I stay in America to be close to the grandkids
I believe guns are evil and should all be banned
But I'm perfectly ok with knives
Axes
Cars
And hands
I believe in freedom of speech
You can say what you feel
But I don't want to hear about Jesus dying on a hill
I believe the government is great and on the right track
But I don't like paying all these taxes
I want my money back
I believe that the church is the most corrupt place around
But that's the first place I run when no other help can be found
I say religion is a crutch only used by the mentally weak
But when I'm really struggling
I ask everybody to pray for me
I say that I love myself and pretend to be so confident
But following others around is how most of my time is spent
I pretend to know it all and not have any spiritual
Mental
Or emotional afflictions
But when it comes down to it
My life is full of all sorts of contradictions

Mind

Ignored all of my life
No real friends
No potential wife
Maybe momma didn't hug me enough
Maybe daddy hugged me too much
It doesn't matter now
I can't even remember
I just know my heart is colder than Alaska in December
Those who've ignored me will finally remember my name
I'm about to have that Tim McVeigh kind of fame
I'm tired of keeping my head down like all the other sheeple
I have never fit in
I'm not like these people
I'm a wolf
And it's time for me to feast
Time to show the world that I really am a beast
Maybe I'll get caught and go out in a blaze of glory
But I really want the chance to tell the world my story
I want them to know why I'm so full of hate and rage
Why I could take those lives regardless of race
Sex
Or age
See
I'm really a coward deep down inside
I'd never join the military
On a hummer I'd never ride
But a room full of people
With nowhere to run
That's more like it
That's my idea of fun
Women and children
Men and boys
Their lives are a game
My guns are my toys
People will be trying to figure me out until the end of time
But they will never understand what was going on in my mind
Because a rational person would've never done what I did

I took pleasure in shooting unarmed adults and kids
I got off on their terror
The blood and screams
Those are the things that make me cream
And you can't explain that
No matter how you try
I can't be fixed
And I deserve to die
But someone will make excuses
I probably won't even go to jail
Even though I've proven that I deserve a special place in hell
Someone will have an agenda
Disguised as being kind
And I'll be allowed to live so they can pretend to study my mind

Just Like You

Why do you hate me
I'm just like you
We share similar dreams and views
We may not see eye to eye on all things
Like what foods are best or what songs to sing
When worshipping God or just to calm down
You may like flying while I prefer to stay on the ground
But that's no reason to hate me
Differences make the rough smooth
If I'm strong where you're weak
Then we can improve
Things
Around us
If we work together
Remember
Two heads are always better than one
Unless
Of course
One of those heads is full of hate
I would love to change your mind
But I think it's too late
Someone taught you that I was supposed to be a certain way
And because of that
In my presence
You refuse to stay
But you can't seem to get me out of your head
I'm not like the lies you were told
Or the books you read
So you search and search
Trying to find a way to support your distorted view
Trying so hard to erase the fact that
I
Am just like you

Thank You

I got up on my own
There was no one to make me
That is one of the benefits of living in a free country
I can put pen to paper whenever I want to write
Without having to worry about keeping certain poems out of sight
I can say whatever I want
Even if it makes someone mad
A blessing that some folks in this world have never had
I didn't have to petition the state for permission to drive
Just pay the fee
Take the test
And keep the DPS worker alive
I get to do so many things that other women aren't allowed to do
And to my God
And all the servicemen
I have to say
Thank you

He risks death or dismemberment every day of his life
She is a soldier first
Before mother or wife
They fight for those who can't fight for themselves
And what they go through they can't even begin to tell
No one knows the pain or the horrors that they've viewed
Yet some attack them for being withdrawn or subdued
While we're sitting in traffic
They're dodging bullets and land mines
Praying that they get the chance to see their family just one more time
We could never repay them for all that they do
But we can take the time out to simply say
Thank you

Don't complain about what they do if you're not willing to take their place
They're the ones that give you the right to complain without hiding your face

Don't be rude when you see them in the store or on the street
They've been through enough
They don't need your contempt when you meet
Don't try to use them for your own selfish gains
They're serving you
Why add to their pain
Don't insult the country that they've given up so much for
They get that when they're deployed
When they get home
They don't want to hear it anymore
Don't ever forget all that they've given up and been through
And never pass up the chance to simply say
Thank You

Free

There is nothing in this life that is completely free
Somebody somewhere is putting out some Em
Oh
En
Ee
Why
Do you sit around just waiting for your next handout
Since when is that what being grown is all about
Last time I checked
An adult takes care of his/her own
Now we've got a bunch of kids playing at being grown
Nobody owes you anything
Not your parents or your kids
Your kids did not choose you even if your parents did
And how can I owe you when we've never even met
Since I don't know you
My not owing you is a safe bet
Yet you cry about how someone else needs to be taking care of you
I'm sorry sweetie but
That's what you're supposed to do
You're not deformed
Disabled
Or mentally handicapped
So why should others foot the bill while you're home taking naps
You're sleeping your life away
Is that what you call livin'
Why don't you try earning something instead of just taking the scraps that you're given
Oh
Wait
I know
That would actually require some work to be done
And you don't want a job
That might cut into all of your fun
You know
The fun of complaining about how you want more

But
You can't afford all of the high prices at the store
Or the gas to get there
And you don't like riding the bus
It's just so hard to get access to all of that free stuff
Listen up kid
Here's a little advice you can take from me
There is nothing in this world that is free

Mr. Ego

Nigga
Just 'cause you got a little local
Or
E-fame
Doesn't mean that you have any type of game
A little confidence is sexy
Yes
That's true
But pure arrogance looks bad on you
I'd rather be with a woman than your sorry ass
If you were the last man on earth
I'd still have to pass
Your attitude can turn my ocean into a desert
You're so damned smug it makes my head hurt
You say you're single because you choose to be
I say that most women think just like me
You may find a girl with no morals or low self-esteem
Which
For a guy like you
Is like living a dream
She'll jump when you say jump
Give your ego constant strokes
But everybody will know that your relationship's a joke
Because you won't care about her
And she won't care about herself
You'll eventually get bored and start looking for someone else
But the good woman that you claim to crave
Would rather be single 'til she's laid in her grave
Than deal with someone like you Mr. Narcissist
She knows she doesn't need you to exist
So keep thinking that you're the second coming
God's gift to the world
Just don't be surprised when the women scatter and you're surrounded by girls

Willie Lynch Nation

It takes a village to raise a child
But for our people
That's no longer in style
You can't tell my child what to do
And instead of helping
I'd rather talk about you
This is nothing new
It's been going on for years
We were taught long ago to focus on our differences and fears
Some lessons may be hard to forget
But I will have the last laugh
You can bet
I know my heritage
I know who I am
I plan on teaching future generations to see the scam
The scam that pits brother against brother
Father against son and daughter against mother
The Civil War was supposedly fought to set us free
Yet everywhere I turn
I see my people still in slavery
How am I a slave
Is the question some ask
Answering that question is a difficult task
But I'll try
I really do want to help
I didn't get this knowledge to keep it to myself
You don't work now and you think that that's just fine
But you're not feeling school either
You don't want to elevate your mind
You say the government owes you since your grandparents weren't paid
I say that's another way to keep you bound
You just got played
You go around saying stuff like
That's just how it is in the hood
But hating on everybody that's able to get out or live good
Talking about how they must think they are hot stuff

When you could've had the same
You just chose not to work enough
But you are just following Massa's orders like a good little slave
Ol' Willie's plan is still working
Even though he's long been cold in his grave
You talk about "the man" and how he's keeping you down
But I don't hear any whips cracking
Or chains making a sound
Do you wonder why they no longer need all of that
It's because the chains are now internal
You carry them under your hat
You're so busy complaining about what the next man has or is trying to get
That you can't even get up and go out to get it
Oh
My bad
You will go get it
Just not your own
You'd rather steal it from the next man when he's not at home
You're stealing from yourself
You and that man are the same
Except
He decided to stop playing Willie's game
He stopped caring about what others said it meant to be black
And looked to our ancestors to see how to act
He didn't even have to go back to the Motherland when we were queens and kings
Because we were strong here
Teaching and preaching
Building
And inventing things
See
Being educated doesn't mean that you're trying to act white
It just means that your eyes have been opened
You've been given new sight
We are NOT an ignorant race
That was an ignorant man's perception
And somewhere along the lines
We bought in to that deception

That the darker your skin
The more ignorant
That you were just heathens and salvation couldn't occur
Until you turned your back on your homeland and embraced the lie
That God's son was born on this earth with blond hair and blue eyes
Which isn't in the Word
At least not the King James' Version
For where they found that lie
I am still searchin'
And that's just one of the millions of lies that they told
Long before our brothers and sisters were stolen
Bought
And sold
Some of you are still buying the original lies
And others
Like
It's perfectly alright for a man to leave his children with their mothers
Or
That being black automatically means being 'hood or a thug
That you're supposed to spend your whole paycheck making it rain at the club
Or the most important thing to have in this life is street cred
That all the good black men are either gay
In jail
On drugs
Or dead
Who said that our children aren't skilled enough to compete
Or the only help for single mothers comes from the government or the street
When you buy into the lies
You're selling the hope of future generations
And ensuring that they'll also grow up in a Willie Lynch nation

Symptoms of a Married Man

He never calls you from his phone
You have never been to his home
He doesn't let you ride in the front seat of his car
And when he does
It isn't very far
He ignores you when you come to his job
And acts as if he's running from the mob
When you get together
It's either your house or a hotel
You want to go to his house
He suddenly doesn't feel well
You ask to meet his family
He quickly tells you no
His boss is throwing a party
But you're not invited to go
You want to visit his church
His car conveniently breaks down
You invite him to yours
But he doesn't like that side of town
The man that you're seeing may not wear a wedding band
But these are the symptoms of a married man

The Disease

This disease is spreading at an alarming rate
Somebody needs to stop this before it's too late
Everyone seems to be catching it
No one is immune
The world is in trouble if we don't find a cure soon
It's not just in America
This thing is worldwide
No one knows for sure just how many have died
Because this disease hides itself well
Only a select few can even tell when they come across a carrier
And they are everywhere
Stocking your food
Teaching your kids
Styling your hair
It has no racial preference
Isn't picky about age
You can catch it at any given life stage
Some have broken free of its effects
And
Like Harriet Tubman
Went back
But when trying to show the cure to others
They were attacked
You see
The only way to beat this disease is to first admit
That there is something wrong
You can only cure the sick
If they acknowledge that they need the medication
We are on the verge of becoming a zombie nation
Because we are medicating people when there's nothing wrong
Turning minds to mush that were once working and strong
But that's just another way that this disease is spread
By convincing the gifted that they're messed up in the head
Add that to what passes for education in the public schools
And of course the media is a most useful tool
Of spreading the disease like a wildfire across dry land
Stupidity is the disease

And it infects boy
Girl
Woman
Man
Somebody needs to stop this before it's too late
So if you're able
Please
EDUCATE EDUCATE EDUCATE

Play

She had been a sweet little girl
The apple of her mother's eye
She couldn't be daddy's little girl
He had long ago said good-bye
And for her
That was the beginning of the end
She searched for that father figure in a continuous stream of boyfriends
She did have nice ones
Every once in a while
Who respected her
Treated her right
And always made her smile
Then there were the others
That were only out for self
Who were constantly attempting to drain her body of its wealth
Her mother tried to warn her
She did all that she could
But the girl was not an only child so it didn't do much good
There was only one mother and quite a few kids
Someone was always quick to undo the good that the mother did
Then there were those on the outside looking in through tainted glass
Who criticized the mother for every little task
She was too strict
She didn't buy the kids enough
The world said she didn't love them because she didn't buy them a lot of stuff
But she gave them what she could
Which was her time and energy
That just didn't seem to be enough
The world just wouldn't let them be
Then one day it happened
What the mother had feared the most
Her daughter disappeared
She simply became a ghost
They searched high and low

Knocked on doors all around
But her little social butterfly was nowhere to be found
Suddenly the folks who had so criticized her before
Finally got the picture and kept showing up at her door
It was too late
The damage had been done
Her child had lost her life because of someone's idea of fun
All those who said that she was too protective and stern
Were secretly happy that
Through her child
A lesson was learned
They hoped that their children would not learn the hard way
That you can lose your life
During what some consider
Play

Lesson Learned

You taught me how to treat you by the way you treated me
By allowing sex to be the only thing that you chose to see
My standing by you
Through the death of your son
Or going through thinking you had another one
Obviously didn't matter that much to you at all
Because I wasn't always available to answer your dick's call
I stood by you when you were hurting
But that didn't mean a thing
Because I wasn't skilled enough to be able to both give head and sing
When your grandmother was sick
I worried like she was mine
I comforted and supported you
Time after time
When your father died
I shed my own silent tears
Knowing how much you regretted all those wasted years
I fought for our love harder than Tyson fought Holyfield
I did my best to show that my love was true and real
But that didn't matter because true love wasn't your choice
The sound of her moans drowned out the sound of my voice
Now you get offended when I say all I want from you is sex
You've shown that it's priority one so I don't understand the texts
That says that you are surprised by my actions
When you've shown me there's nothing more important than sexual satisfaction
You taught me not to get my heart involved
Love is a wasted emotion
Just make sure I have some clean towels close
And KY warming lotion
It took me a while
But I promise I finally understand
You want a woman to hold your dick not your heart or your hand
I finally stopped looking with my heart
So a piece of meat is all that I see
You taught me how to treat you by the way you treated me

Stone

You showed me how I should be treated
Yes
That's true
Then showed me that falling in love is something I don't want to do
I didn't know you weren't ready when I gave you my heart
I wish that I had known the risks from the start
I would've backed up
I would've walked away
Regardless to how much you begged me to stay
I tried to walk away
But you said you needed me
It was all a game
I just couldn't see that you didn't love me
It was all just a show
Why you chose me
I still don't know
You had other options
I wasn't the only one
But my heart was the target chosen by your deceptive gun
I enjoyed the flowers and candy
All the sweet gifts
But I'd give it all back
If this pain would lift
I realize now that there's a good reason why I had shut down
And it's that love is the circus
Where I always get clowned
See
How to be treated is only half of the lesson that I learned
The other half was painful
Which is why
To stone
My heart has been turned

Melting Pot

America was supposed to be a melting pot
But I think the cook must've gotten shot
Or maybe he's over in the corner getting high
Whoever said equal opportunity for all
Was a lie
They judge you on skin tone
Or where you were born
By the clothes you wear
Or your grandmother might've worn
It's better to be a criminal
Or political refugee
Than a law-abiding citizen in this
So-called free country
There's racism
Classism
And all sorts of other crap
This isn't a melting pot
It's a fire trap
And the ones being burned
Are this country's backbone
Being made to feel that being American also means being wrong
We deport folks for expired visas who were following the rules
But criminals get free healthcare
And access to schools
I'm a little confused
And I'm not trying to be a jerk
I just want to know why we throw out the ones who actually want to work
While keeping the murderers
Rapists
And crooks
And yes
It is indeed as bad as it looks
This country was built
On lies and genocide
Shady backroom deals
And crooked laws

Applied
To any group
Thought to be too large
By the select few who want to remain in charge
See
When you melt things together
You get something new
But we haven't even been able to make a decent stew
We've got the ingredients
They've all been laid out
But either the recipe's gone
Or the cook has no clout
Or maybe
The fire just got too hot
Either way
We are nowhere near a melting pot

Internalized

What bothers me the most about racism
Isn't what you see
It's how it affects those who don't look like me
Like the guy named Juan
Who says call me Joe
Because he doesn't want to be viewed as Mexican any mo'
Or the girl who refuses to speak Spanish
And gets mad if you ask
Who speaks slowly
With no accent
Just so she can pass
Or all of the people who changed their last name
Just so they wouldn't be looked at the same
As the guy whose last name
Is hard to pronounce
Because perception
Not reality
Is what seems to count
I feel bad for the people who don't look like me
Who feel the need to hide their ethnicity
It's obvious that God created the different races of man
Why so many want to be the same one
I really don't understand
Don't you know that no matter how much of their stuff you have
When you're not around
They still talk about you
And laugh
At your silly attempts to be something that you're not
Take pride in your heritage
It's all that you've got
Nobody is pure anything these days anyway
If your ancestors could speak to you
What would they say
Would they be proud of the way you've tossed them aside
Of how you've conformed so much that you have no self-pride
There's only one Heaven
And no separated parts of Hell

So enjoy who you are
I mean
You may as well
Embrace who you are
Don't put a part of you on the shelf
The worst racist in the world
Is the one who hates himself

The Journey

How did I get here
Who trapped me
When did I forget all the things that I wanted to be
I wanted to make a difference
To change the world
But somewhere
I lost the dreams of that little girl
She was lost in the shuffle
Along with her dreams
Her spirit starved and beaten
While the world ignored its screams
She changed as she grew old
Her light went dim
Her heart grew cold
But there was a spark inside that refused to die
No matter how much she screamed
Or how many tears she cried
That spark would flare up every now and then
Until life stepped in to smother it yet again
But that spark was put there by a Higher Power
And couldn't be put out
Not by pain
Bitterness
Anger
Or doubt
Those things actually fed the flames
They helped them grow strong
She needed to release the fire
Or it would consume her before long
So she picked up her pen and began to write
Releasing the things that had kept her up at night
She released things that had been hidden for years
Sometimes pausing to wipe away the tears
That flowed as freely as the ink onto the page
Freeing herself and opening her cage
She no longer felt restless
Her purpose returned

She appreciated her age
And the lessons she'd learned
She realized everything had happened at the right time
She could see the purpose
That the plan was divine
No longer restless
Now full of desire and energy
So full of life and enjoying her journey

Scared

We say the children are the future
And I'm really scared
Because once most kids become adults
They are so unprepared
Their parents were little more than kids themselves
And just didn't know
Or maybe they were the type that didn't know how to show
Love and affection
Those are things that a child needs
Not a bunch of junk that only increases their greed
Parents who give their children everything without it being earned
Are depriving their kids of an important lesson that they really need to learn
That lesson is imperative and ranks right up there with shelter and meals
The lesson is that you have to work for what you want
No matter how you feel
Food isn't free
The bills don't pay themselves
And the house does not get cleaned by helpful little elves
Those things are worked for
Somebody broke a sweat
If you don't understand that
Then you're not grown yet
Another lesson being missed by the children of this age
Is that when you act like an animal
You will end up in a cage
Or to put it in a more politically correct fashion
There are consequences to your actions
Spankings are illegal
Discipline is taboo
That doesn't prepare them for what they can go through
No is a word unspoken
Rejection is never felt
They aren't learning to play with the cards they were dealt
If this is our future
Then I am very afraid

Because they're used to winning
Even if they've never played
A caterpillar has to work to build its own cocoon
The struggle gives the butterfly its beauty
It can't be released too soon
Yet we send our children into the world thoroughly unprepared
If these children are our future
Then I am really
And truly
Scared

Reminder

You think you've won
But you'll soon learn
How will you act when it's your turn
When you're on the outside
Looking in
And someone else is lying next to him
It was fun for you
And you enjoyed the chase
But in a few months
How will rejection taste
Things will end the same way they began
And you'll play confused as if you don't understand
But there's already a voice in the back of your mind
Replaying words that you've heard a million times
If they'll cheat with you then they'll cheat on you
You'll soon become a living witness that these words are true
How will you feel when those tables are turned
Will you remember the lesson that you've learned
Or will you continue trying to hone your home wrecker skills
Constantly targeting those with loose morals and weak wills
One day you'll meet your match
And want to leave the game
But karma will step in and they won't feel the same
They'll see you like you've seen all the rest
Just another number on their list of relationship conquests
So go ahead and laugh
Keep thinking that you've won
There will come a day when you're reminded of all the dirt you've done

Elite

Wake up people
Don't you see what's going on
If we can't come together
We'll fall apart before long
We keep fighting each other
Some can't see past the hate
And while we're distracted
The wolves have just walked in the gate
They say it's not about race
And that might be true
Because they're doing to their own
The same thing they're doing to you
See
It's about power
And those little pieces of paper
If you don't have that
Then
To them
Your life is worth less than vapor
As long as the powers that be can keep us fighting amongst ourselves
They can keep stealing from us
Because we buy every lie that they tell
You just want to see the colors
While I'm looking at the entire picture
And even though I know this has to happen
That it was foretold in the scripture
Doesn't mean that I'm going to sit back and be silent
Even though I know that
To silence me
Some might get violent
But the Great Shepherd gave me something to do
So I am going to do it until my life is through
Educate the masses
Warn them of things to come
Round up My sheep
Don't miss anyone

Those were my instructions
Given before my first breath
And I am going to follow them
Until I don't have any left
I'm trying to help somebody live before they die
To finally see the truth
And stop believing the lie
The lie that you can look at a man and see what is within
Just by the way that he dresses
Or the color of his skin
They know that if we come together
We'll do more than just marching through the streets
There are more of us than them
And we'd easily overthrow the governing elite

Her Story

She had never known the love of a man
Her father hadn't been around
And all the other males in her life
Only wanted to put her down
She was too skinny
Too fat
Not enough of this
Too much of that
They loved her lips
Both top and bottom
But quickly disappeared as soon as they got 'em
Or didn't get 'em
For the times she said no
Either way
This girl's life seemed to have a revolving do'
Men came in one day
And were out the next
Never offering love
Only wanting sex
In her mind
Her loneliness would always last
Then she met a man
That was a complete contrast
To all the men she had met before
He made her yearn for something more
This was a setup for a disaster to occur
Because he was married
And didn't want her
At least
Not in a romantic way
Although he enjoyed bringing joy to her day
Friendship is all he would ever give
But she thought that
Without him
She could not live
Infatuation turned to obsession over time
He started to worry about her state of mind

He tried what he could
And gently explained
That it was never his intention to cause her pain
He only wanted to bring some light into her dark life
But not to the point of leaving his wife
She begged and pleaded
Screamed and cried
She even blamed him
And said that he lied
But in her heart
She knew she was wrong
He had done nothing to lead her on
And it hurt him for her to accuse him so
But she was obsessed
And didn't want to let go
So she tried to guilt him into staying instead
Saying he was her life
And without him she'd be dead
He became nervous at her trying to give him God's glory
And decided it was time for his chapter to end
So she could continue her story

The Rule

I am NOT the exception
I am the rule
You don't have to be white to excel in school
And being black doesn't affect your brain
Although it does make those who aren't act kinda strange
When you show any sort of promise
Their own ignorance is obvious
To everyone but them
They show it through their actions and words
Their thought process is absurd
If the darker you get the dumber you are
Then tanning salon owners shouldn't get that far
All beaches should be permanently closed
And no one should wear revealing clothes
Bikinis should be obsolete
If dark and dumb always meet
And if big lips and Ebonics go hand in hand
Then why is Hollywood collagen land
Where lips are larger than car doors
On Cadillacs
But big lips are only wrong on blacks
Right
It's cool for folks who glow at night
Or lack melanin
Since when do we learn through our skin
And are you sure that ALL of your kin
Has European ancestry
I bet if you shake your family tree
You'll find someone who looks like me
And they were probably smart too
So
Here's what I need you to do
Understand that grades don't mean much
When the teacher doesn't care or is out of touch
And statistics are manipulated everyday
So people will see things a certain way
Check your "facts" and where they came from

And if
On your list of "educated blacks" I'm the only one
Count up the total number you know
Then hopefully
Common sense will show
That the reason your list is so small
Is that you don't really know any blacks at all

www.ingramcontent.com/pod-product-compliance
Lightning Source LLC
Chambersburg PA
CBHW021328190426
43193CB00040B/633